THE WORLD IN YOUR KITCHEN

'*The World in Your Kitchen* cook-book is very welcome. My imagination will be given a very necessary fillip by this international gathering of recipes.'
Glenda Jackson

'This colourful book demonstrates the amazing world-wide diversity of vegetarian ingredients and shows how just about every non-Western culture in the world has developed healthy non-meat cuisine. *The World in Your Kitchen* is packed with handy tips and nutritional advice and I wholeheartedly recommend it.'
Jane Brophy BSc SRD,
Nutritionist/Research and Information Officer,
The Vegetarian Society of the United Kingdom

'Troth Wells makes a valuable contribution to moving us all toward a more sustainable world with *The World in Your Kitchen*. Reducing consumption of meat is a personal contribution we can all make as we strive to end world hunger.'
Marilyn Borchardt,
Institute for Food and Development Policy/Food First,
San Francisco, USA

'If you believe we are one world and that our survival depends on inter-dependency rather than independency then, in terms of food and cooking, this is the book for you. How vegetarianism here affects those at the other side of the world, how ingredients we've always taken for granted are produced, why different world cuisines have evolved, and the most delicious recipes which even a novice can make – it's all in *The World in Your Kitchen*. In other words, I recommend it!'
Julie Christie

'*The World in Your Kitchen* is a delightful book. Its fare tempts the palate, expands our global awareness – all while helping us to eat more healthfully and ecologically. What else could one wish for? There are recipes for all who want to enjoy the many varied pleasures of our ever smaller planet!'
Frances Moore Lappé,
author of best-seller Diet for a Small Planet

Two women and baskets, Nepal. *Photo: Thomas L. Kelly.*

THE WORLD IN YOUR KITCHEN

BY

Troth Wells

Front cover photos: Fruits and beans, *Mark Mason.* Boy, Brazil,
Sarah Errington, Hutchison Photo Library.
Back cover photo: Market traders by vegetable stall, Goa, India, *David Hanson/Tony Stone Worldwide.*
Endpapers: Ingredients, *Mark Mason.*

The New Internationalist Vegetarian Food Book
The World in Your Kitchen *Vegetarian recipes from Africa, Asia, the Caribbean and Latin America and the Middle East for Western kitchens*
First published in Great Britain by
New Internationalist Publications Ltd,
55 Rectory Road, Oxford, OX4 1BW.

Copyright © Troth Wells/New Internationalist 1993
and individuals contributing recipes. All rights reserved.

Copyright © For photographs and illustrations rests with the individual
photographers/agencies and illustrators.

Design and typesetting by New Internationalist.

Printed by South China Printing Co. (1988) Ltd.
New Territories, Hong Kong.

BRITISH LIBRARY CATALOGUING-IN-PUBLICATION DATA.
A catalogue record for this book is available from the British Library.
ISBN 1 869 847 15 6

New Internationalist Publications Ltd
Registered Office: 55 Rectory Road,
Oxford OX4 1BW, UK.

FOREWORD

ONE of the things I like best about vegetarian food is that most of the raw ingredients come in packaging you can eat. And even if the packaging should be inedible – think of a pineapple – chop it up a bit and it will help on the compost heap. Waste not, want not, as my mother used to say.

I also like the taste of vegetarian food. My son, however, does not. 'Ugh, healthy food' is his usual response, accompanied by a suitably disgusted facial expression. So this **New Internationalist** contribution to the cook-book shelf is very welcome. My attempt to delude my son into believing that Bean Casserole is really Shepherd's Pie, simply by adding a generous layer of mashed potato, was rumbled long ago. My imagination will be given a very necessary fillip by this international gathering of recipes – hopefully my son will gain a liking for a more balanced diet.

Of course the majority of the world's mothers worry not about balanced diets for their daughters and sons but whether they can provide them simply with enough food. And not because their children are picky eaters or voraciously greedy, but because poverty, individual and national, is the only life they have ever known. And unless the rich world begins to take less of the world's finite resources and give more to the developing world in aid and practical know-how, without strings, poverty is all the majority of our fellow human beings will ever know.

Trying to explain the basic inequity of one third of the world using 80 per cent of resources while two-thirds of the world is trying desperately to manage on the remaining 20 per cent, is what the **New Internationalist** magazine is about.

So this isn't just another cook-book. The recipes are imaginative and tasty and nothing has had to be killed to form a part of any dish. Vegetarian food is 'good for you' but buying this book will help **New Internationalist** to continue the work of such vital importance, not only to the developing countries, but to all of us.

There is only one planet, one world and the accident of birth should not deny anyone the right to fully participate in sharing or caring for this small blue ball in the middle of a vast black space.

Buy it, enjoy it.

Acknowledgments

First of all, thank you to everyone who helped make the previous NI Food Book a success, because without that we would not have embarked on this vegetarian follow-up, The World in Your Kitchen.

Despite the pressures of recently becoming a Member of Parliament, Glenda Jackson still found the time to write the Foreword to this book and I am very grateful to her for this.

The book is published in co-operation with Virago, with thanks to Ruth Petrie there for her enthusiasm for the project.

The centerpiece of any cook-book is the recipes and I would like to thank Julie Christie for her contributions, and also the other NI friends and subscribers who sent them in including Phoebe Omondi, Nalin Wijesekera, Beng Tuan, Sophia Twum-Barima, Meghna Guhathakurta and Shahidul Alam, Peter Stockton, and Mary Namakando. These recipes often came embellished with detail about local ingredients or places which I have tried to incorporate into the introductory paragraphs above each dish.

Reading the letters and recipes was the easy part: next came the testing time of cooking the combinations of spices, pulses, vegetables, nuts, fruits and grains into the various dishes. This was a painstaking process, what with getting the measurements right and the tastes harmonious. But it was fun as well. Many thanks to Dinyar Godrej and William Beinart for their wisdom, culinary skills and enthusiasm. The guinea-pigs for our efforts deserve a mention too – Ann, Gabriel, Katy, Rebecca and Bart – who munched their way from frijoles to fritters with helpful if forthright comments.

After the recipe testing came the writing, often a solitary and difficult task. But in this I was helped by William Beinart and colleagues at New Internationalist, especially Chris Brazier, Dexter Tiranti and David Ransom who made thoughtful comments on the text. Thanks are due also to Jane Brophy of the UK Vegetarian Society for advice on the Nutrition Guide.

Next was the design and production stage. Many thanks to NI designers Alan Hughes and Kate Stott whose professionalism has made working on this book such a pleasure. Jim Turner produced high-quality dummy spreads and Clive Offley did some fine sketches at the drop of a hat. Dinyar Godrej shared with me the considerable task of proof-reading which he undertook with relish and great attention to detail.

New Internationalist is a co-operative and it is hard to think of anyone who has not been involved in some way at some stage: so thank you to Vanessa Baird, Chris Brazier, Wayne Ellwood, Alan Hughes, Jana Mahalingam, Guy Montgomery, Gill Moore, Clive Offley, David Ransom, James Rowland, Debbie Simms, Jane Sluman, Sue Shaw, Kate Stott, Richard Swift, Dexter Tiranti and Jim Turner.

CONTENTS

THE WORLD IN YOUR KITCHEN

For most people in the world, meat is a luxury – and that is the way it should stay if we are to feed everyone. Cutting out or cutting down on meat-eating would release land to grow food for humans. Looking at some of the reasons why meat is so central,
Troth Wells *explains why now is the time to push it to the side of our plates and make way for the nutritious wealth and diversity of plant foods.*

'MY (vegetarian) diet is strange to most Zambians,' Mary Namakando told me during lunch at a seminar for African journalists held a couple of years ago in Harare. 'Africans are big meat eaters when they can get it,' she went on, 'And they find it totally alien for one of their kind to eat "grass" as they contemptuously call a vegetarian diet.'

Talking with Mary was very helpful, for at that point I was just starting work on this **New Internationalist Vegetarian Food Book**, 'The World in your Kitchen'. The issue of vegetarianism had arisen with the first **NI Food Book**, published in 1990. Although this was well received, one criticism that rang loud was that it included meat and fish recipes. Some people felt that the **NI** should not advocate meat-eating, for reasons ranging from concern about sustainable farming and feeding the world, to concern over animal rights, protecting the environment, and, yes, the role of capitalism and patriarchy as well.

The next few pages look at these issues and try to explain why people eat meat in the first place. This helps put in context the arguments for reducing or ending meat-eating. And after that comes a little about the rich store of plant food available in the world, some of which features as recipes in this book.

Many of the dishes were sent in by contributors and subscribers to the **NI** magazine and reflect the variety of vegetarian meals from Africa, Asia, the Middle East and Latin America. These are the unsung heroic dishes, the nutritious stuff of daily life for millions of people. But what better way to start a meal than avocado pear, spiced with lime juice and chili, and made into the creamy Central American dip, *guacamole?* Then there is a delicious cashew nut curry from Sri Lanka and *aprapransa*, a Ghanaian black-eyed bean stew flavored with palm-nut butter.

In Kenya I came across some of the nicest *samosas* I have ever tasted, and also encountered *irio*, a one-pot dish of corn/maize, beans or peas and greens that's easy to make. One of my favorites when I lived for a time in Malaysia was *gado-gado*, a cooked vegetable dish topped with a spicy peanut sauce. For desserts, I delight in the Middle Eastern pastries such as the Tunisian *samsa* (even though I'm no great shakes as a pastry-maker) and the simple mango dish *aam ras* from India. And for tea or a snack try a molasses-dark gingerbread from Jamaica or rum cake from Mauritius – see the recipe section for a mouth-watering wealth of non-meat dishes.

For although by no means all the people in these countries are vegetarians, the plain fact is that they do not eat meat with as much frequency or in such large quantities as in the North. It may not always be available, and can cost a lot, so it is usually provided for special occasions such as festivals or marriages. Nigeria's per-capita meat consumption is 14 pounds a year and China's 50 compared with the UK's 163 pounds, Australia's 247, and the US's 266. In India people eat as little as two pounds of meat each a year.

Feeding the world

Could the world be fed on the West's meat and dairy centered diet? It seems not. Former UK ambassador to the United Nations Sir Crispin Tickell noted that if 35 per cent of our calories came from animal products – as in North America now – then the world would only be able to sustain 2.5 billion people. But if everyone became vegetarian and the food was equally distributed, the world could support at least six billion people (world population in 1992 was 5.5 billion but all too many of these people were undernourished). So if we are serious about reducing world hunger, we have to take vegetarianism seriously.

If you think about it, feeding grains and beans to animals is a circuitous way of producing food for humans. It is also wasteful and inefficient. In the US, livestock eat 145 million tons of grain and soy a year to produce only 21 million tons of animal products. 'How would you like to buy 145 gallons of gasoline for your car and only be able to use 21 gallons?' asks Gary Null, author of *The Vegetarian Handbook*. The average person in the United States consumes around 2,000 pounds of grain each year, yet all but 150 pounds is in the form of animal foods.

With this in mind, I wondered what it would be like if the Western world was the other way about. If, instead of vegetarians being the minority, they were the majority and meat-eaters had to justify their position. In that case, it might seem bizarre that in the UK in one year people chomp their way through almost four million cattle and calves, 19.5 million sheep, 14.5 million pigs and 505 million chickens. For each person in their lifetime that amounts to 7 or 8 cattle, 36 sheep, 36 pigs, 750 poultry birds plus some rabbits and game.

In the United States, even greater numbers of animals are consumed. Over his or her lifetime the average citizen eats 11 cows and 4 veal calves, 3 lambs, 43 pigs, 1,107 chickens, 45 turkeys and 861 fish. Put another way, each of the US's 250 million or so people consumes over 250 pounds of meat and poultry each year. And many of these animals, as seen earlier, eat grains and soy protein that could feed people directly.

If everybody adopted a low-meat or vegetarian diet, the combined surplus of both grain and legumes such as beans would be available as food for the world's hungry people. Reducing our own meat-eating is an important first step, giving a strong signal to meat producers, marketing boards and governments that as consumers we do not want food to be squandered in this way.

Of mice and men

Why do we eat meat in the first place? And how does that yearning for a steak or burger affect our environment, our health and nutrition, and the animals themselves?

All over the world, meat has a central position in people's minds, if not actually in their meals. Among people such as the !Kung of the Kalahari, or the Yanomami in the Amazon, meat (from hunting) has been the most prized food, even though it only provides between 15 and 40 per cent of people's nutrition – the rest comes from foraging in the case of the !Kung and from cultivation in the case of the Yanomami.

'Whenever my father brought back meat,' recalls Nisa, a !Kung woman, 'I'd greet him: "Ho, Daddy's coming home with meat!" And I felt thankful for everything and there was nothing that made my heart unhappy.'

In the West also meat is often linked with a sense of well-being, as in this letter to the UK *Meat Trades Journal*:

'For three hours on Sunday the smell of (pork) cooking practically drove us wild. When we finally sat down at the table, all the troubles of the week seemed to drift away at the prospect of a delicious family lunch… My family left the table feeling well fed and happy.'

Orde Eliason/Link

Men's game: hunting prowess was linked with men's dominance and perceived role as providers, even though trophies like this springhare were only a small part of a family's food – most came from women's gathering or cultivation.

Meat-eating is also connected with men's dominant role in most societies – through their perceived role as providers. 'The supply of animals, and thus of meat,' explains anthropologist Nick Fiddes, 'has tended… to be controlled primarily by the wealthier, the more skilled, the more powerful, the central actors in the human drama.' I would add that, aside from 'more skilled', this is a description of men in general.

This is the case, whether in non-industrial societies like that of the !Kung or in highly industrialized countries like the US. All through history, all over the world, meat is bound up with expressions of maleness, from prowess in hunting to skill with a carving knife. Meat has become an especially 'male' food, and if there is a shortage then women and children make do with 'lesser' foods like eggs. When women eat meat, it is often at the dispensation of their men or husbands. In parts of Indonesia, for example, flesh food is viewed as the property of men, and is distributed to households according to the men in them. The system of distribution thus reinforces male prestige in society.

Foods associated with women – such as vegetables – are seen as second class. 'Just as it is thought that a woman cannot make it on her own,' notes feminist writer Carol Adams, 'So we think that vegetables cannot make a meal on their own – despite the fact that meat is only secondhand vegetables.'

But what about men who reject meat? In the West, they may be thought suspect because they appear to be challenging the masculine role, or rejecting an aspect of maleness. '(People) seemed to automatically assume that because I was vegetarian then I must be gay,' explained one man, in Nick Fiddes' book *Meat*. He added: 'I'm sure it was because of the thing about meat being a sort of virility symbol.'

The idea that you are what you eat, that meat and especially red meat (albeit derived from a placid herbivore like the cow) makes you tough and powerful is still an important influence. Meat-eating has been a potent symbol of power over the wilderness, but also over women and other races too. It has a fascinating history.

At every season, turn, turn, turn

There is something faintly humorous about the way some people have twisted and turned to rationalize the control over animals which led to regular meat-eating.

You probably know the kind of thing: in the Garden of Eden, Eve and Adam are vegetarians. After the Fall, the unhappy pair start eating meat for their sins and God says all living things are there for humans. Meanwhile, away from the Creation tale, it appears that the Hebrews were indeed vegetarians and did not become meat-eaters until after the Flood, when God said they could eat living things too.

In the East, by contrast, religion was the spur to vegetarianism. Buddha commanded his devotees not to indulge 'a

Cakes and ale: everyday foods in ancient Egypt included vegetables such as onions, and bread, washed down with ale.

voracity that involves the slaughter of animals.' For Hindus, the epic *Mahabharata* poem laid down the guiding principle that 'Those who desire to possess good memory, beauty, long life with perfect health, and physical, moral and spiritual strength should abstain from animal foods'.

In one of the earliest settled societies, the Sumerians commonly ate barley-cake, beans, onions and ale, with fish from time to time. Cattle were not usually slaughtered until the end of their lives. Later, ordinary Egyptians mainly survived on flat-bread, onions and ale. In Classical Greece, the hilly land was stripped of trees for houses, ship-building and charcoal. The eroded hills supported little livestock. So the Greeks also did not eat much meat, and protein-rich barley was considered the most prestigious food, awarded to victors in the Eleusinian Games.

It wasn't difficult therefore for Pythagoras and Plutarch to be vegetarians, and their philosophizing about it may in part have been a rationalization of their lack of access to meat. But they were certainly impassioned in their rhetoric. Here's

Plutarch, from his *Moralia*:

'Why do you belie the earth, as if it were unable to feed and nourish you? Does it not shame you to mingle murder and blood with her beneficent fruits? Other carnivora you call savage and ferocious – lions, tigers and serpents... yet for them murder is the only means of sustenance! Whereas to you it is superfluous luxury and crime!'

Aristotle on the other hand, who believed that 'animals exist for the sake of man', probably had a stash of goats somewhere to provision his kitchen.

Bread, porridge, vegetables, wine and occasionally fish were the Romans' basic foods. 'The Roman army conquered the world on a vegetarian diet,' says historian Will Durant. 'Caesar's troops complained when the corn ran out and they had to eat meat.'

Meat-centered Europe

'Human civilization...was virtually synonymous with the conquest of nature,' explains historian Keith Thomas. All over the world, people chopped down trees and killed animals. But the scale of ecological plunder that arose out of Europe was unique. It stemmed directly from Aristotle's belief that animals as well as plants existed to serve humanity.

Between ancient and modern times came the years that laid the foundations for today's high meat consumption in the West. It is this Western consumption which is of prime concern because we eat so much more meat than developing countries, and our intensive methods of livestock-rearing are being exported to other parts of the world.

In medieval Europe, the Bible was interpreted as buttressing the view that nature existed for humans – who, after all, had been created in God's image and therefore were superior to all other living things. Later, seventeenth-century French philosopher René Descartes reflected the rise of mechanistic science with the view that animals were automata: like clocks, they were capable of complex behaviour but not of sensation. They had no minds or souls.

These ideas were seized upon not least because they justified the way animals were already treated as they gave up their fur, wool, milk, draught power and meat. The ox and the horse were early harnessed to European ploughs, giving the region a powerful advantage that would later count over Chinese, Aztec and Inca societies.

At this time, England and the Netherlands had the highest ratios of domesticated animals to people in Europe. As horses

Carving out control: meat became a symbol of male power, both over the family and over other nations.

replaced oxen in English plough-shafts, oxen were used increasingly as food. And although country people mainly lived on cheese, milk and roots, it was a different picture in London. Here they ate more 'good beef and mutton in one month than all Spain, Italy and a part of France in a whole year,' observed writer Henry Peacham in 1667. In 1748 a Swedish visitor noted that England was different from any other country in that meat formed the centerpiece of the main meal of the day.

It was during this period that 'the roast beef of England' became a national symbol, embellished with the ritual of carving at table, and imbued with ideas of male dominance, both over the family and over other people and races.

This beef and supremacy link in nineteenth-century England was so overt that the English, who ate six times as much beef as the French, considered that this 'distinguished the brave and brawny English soldiers from the puny, snivelling Frenchmen' in the Napoleonic wars.

The British population's expansion in the eighteenth century offered a challenge to farmers and breeders. The gentry responded by producing stately prize bulls, thought to be a fitting representation of their own breeding and dignity. At this period animals were fed on pasture grass and as breeder Robert Bakewell put it 'an excellent cow or sheep was the best machine for converting herbage into money.'

But even then people were objecting to the way animals were treated. The 'shambles' or slaughter-houses, carcasses suspended, were in the high street for all to see and smell. The prize cattle paraded at Smithfield cattle show in London were so enormous that some could barely totter around the ring. In 1800, 500,000 people petitioned against producing such over-grown beasts.

There had always been people opposed to animal slaughter. Some disapproved of the killing of animals for sport or for use in vivisection, while condoning the taking of animal life for food or in self-defence. Others were early advocates of vegetarianism. Leonardo da Vinci, Shakespeare, Francis Bacon, Aphra Behn, Alexander Pope, Voltaire and Percy Shelley eschewed meat-eating, as later did Leo Tolstoy and George Bernard Shaw.

In his *Notes*, Leonardo da Vinci wrote: 'I have from an early age abjured the use of meat, and the time will come when men such as I will look upon the murder of animals as they now look upon the murder of men.'

Shelley wrote on vegetarianism, incorporating his views into works such as *Queen Mab* and, here, in *Prometheus Unbound*: 'I wish no living thing to suffer pain.' The title of his essay *A Vindication of Natural Diet* deliberately evoked the title of Mary Wollstonecraft's feminist work, *A Vindication of the Rights of Woman*.

In Britain from about 1790, a coherent vegetarian movement began to develop with Joseph Ritson and John Oswald among the early activists. Oswald, author of *The Cry of Nature* in 1791, had been converted to vegetarianism by Hindus he met while serving in the army in India. Others included the aptly named William Cowherd and William Metcalfe who extended their ideas to North America, leading to more converts. In 1847 the Vegetarian Society of Great Britain was founded but vegetarianism remained the preoccupation of a handful of intellectuals.

All the while, of course, millions of Buddhists, Hindus and followers of the philosophies of Yoga and Jainism were eating very well without animal products. 'Hold fast to vegetarianism and abstain from taking life,' was an early Confucian saying, while Mohandas Gandhi, born in 1869, wrote: 'I do not regard flesh-food as necessary for us at any stage and under any clime…'

But as the nineteenth century drew to a close, meat was fast becoming big business in the West. On the American plains and in the Australian outback, cows and sheep grazed in increasing numbers. This was one aspect of settlerdom, as people staked their claim to land by putting their animals on it – so displacing anyone who might have been there already. Improved rail transport and refrigeration meant animals and meat could be moved in larger quantities to centers of slaughter, packaging and distribution.

In 1906 when Upton Sinclair exposed the grim conditions for workers in the Chicago meat industry in his book, *The Jungle*, he inadvertently also graphically exposed the grim conditions for pigs as they were hoisted aloft, 'dangling by a foot and kicking in frenzy', on the production line for slaughter. 'I aimed at the public's heart and by accident hit it in the stomach,' he commented ruefully. That vicarious visit to the slaughterhouse for his readers was shocking as it brought them face to face with the reality of the way meat was produced – and is still produced now.

Today we have a meat industry which parodies the automobile factory, with dis-assembly lines for animals. Descartes' idea of animals as automata, re-iterated by Robert Bakewell the cattle breeder, is given a fearful resonance in our factory farms, where increasing numbers of animals live force-fed lives right up to their untimely deaths.

Raynes/FAO

Reaping the facts: worldwide, a third of the world's grain is grown for livestock and in the US some 90 per cent of the corn, oats and barley goes down animal gullets.

Cattle ranching in cleared rainforest, Brazil. *Photo: Ed Parker/Still Pictures.*

Down on the (factory) farm

Forget the green fields and the rugged farmer chewing on a straw as he surveys his stock. Farming isn't like that any more. It is dark sheds and big bucks. Today, 20 large corporations control poultry production in the United States. Companies and business people that have no connection with agriculture own over half the US farmland. Ham may come from communications company IT & T, turkeys from the Greyhound Bus Corporation and beef from an oil company. Just four corporations, including Montfort and Excel, control 80 per cent of the slaughterhouses. Food retail giants Swift and Pillsbury for example control an estimated 90 per cent of the chicken market.

We are talking about mass production. To obtain more meat or eggs from animals, humans have applied technology as clinically as they would to speed up a computer's processes or to produce more dishwashers. But animals are not like a semi-conductor or a piece of pressed steel. They feel – and they suffer.

To process animals into meat we pump them with hormones to promote growth and antibiotics to prevent disease. In the chicken and veal sheds we strictly regulate light, heat and movement so that the animals do not 'waste' their food by expending energy. Chickens for the pot ('broilers') are raised to killing-weight in 42 days in the UK, but this is not fast enough to compete: in other European Community countries and in the US, they reach killing-weight in just 35 days, with the help of growth-promoting drugs.

Meat producers rely on grains such as corn/maize, soy beans and cassava/manioc to provide a protein-rich diet for their imprisoned stock. It takes ten pounds of grain to produce one pound of beef; three pounds to yield one pound of poultry. And a good deal of this food for our cows, pigs and chickens is imported from developing countries.

Your land is our land, still

About two hours' drive from Davao in the southern Philippines, Esperanza Martinez has her small farm. Like her neighbors she used to grow rice and corn to eat, with *abacca* (Manila hemp) as a crop grown for cash. Then things changed. The US fruit conglomerate Dole came along and made her an offer she could not refuse to plant bananas for export on her farm. Today Esperanza is in debt to Dole for fertilizers and pesticides she had to use on their bananas. She has no home-grown food, and no money to buy any.

Banana boat-load: Dominica's bananas for export use land that could grow food for local people.

Philip Wolmuth

Esperanza's tale is another aspect of the West's continuing domination of the Third World. We encourage developing countries to grow food such as bananas for us and fodder for our animals instead of producing food first for themselves. We also encourage countries to raise livestock there to be shipped as meat for our tables.

The root of the world's hunger problem is the misuse of land resources. Growing crops such as bananas, cocoa, cotton and soybeans for export, mainly to the rich countries of the North, does not help feed local people.

Worldwide, over one third of all grain is grown to feed livestock. 'European animal production is annually fed 22 million tons of imported feedstuffs,' says Nick Fiddes. In Senegal, for instance, 30 per cent of cultivated land is used to grow feed for this purpose. Even at the height of the 1985 famine, Ethiopia exported protein that would have fed around one million people annually. Cassava/manioc from Thailand and soy beans from Brazil also help put the beef into European cattle.

For another example of the way the West's demand for meat affects Third World food supplies, look at cattle-rearing in Latin America. Here, although production has risen in some regions, local consumption has fallen. This was because meat can be sold to the United States or the European Community at far higher prices than local people could afford. In Brazil's drought-stricken north-east, for instance, wealthy landlords have reserved the best land for cash crops and beef cattle. This soaks up what little water there is, leaving local landless Brazilians thirsty and impoverished.

In a different part of that same country, in Amazonia, rainforest (and the people who lived there) has been cleared to make way for new inhabitants – more than eight million cattle. But, according to Nick Hildyard of *The Ecologist* magazine, production is inefficient and would never have been undertaken on such a large scale without hefty handouts from the Brazilian Government, the World Bank and other development banks. The cost of our steaks, hamburgers and petfood from such cattle is high. It has been calculated that when rainforest is cleared for raising cattle the cost of each hamburger produced in the first year is about half a ton of mature forest. As each tree crashes down, local people's environment is diminished, species are lost, and we lose another sponge that has soaked up the worst offender in the Greenhouse Gas Gang, carbon dioxide.

What a waste…

We have seen that large-scale livestock rearing can directly affect the environment – by cutting down rainforest and taking over land that could grow food for people. Meat production draws heavily on other resources, too. Inputs of antibiotics, food and water have a high cost. For example, it takes around 60 gallons of water to produce one pound of wheat, but 2,500 gallons to yield one pound of beef.

This is not all. With intensive farming methods we get mountains of manure and rivers of urine to be disposed of. This nitrogenous waste can leach into streams and groundwater, contaminating human drinking water.

Pulsing with protein

People may abhor many of the processes involved in meat procurement, and yet still eat it. Why? For some, it is simply because they know we need to eat protein, and learned at school that protein means meat, cheese, eggs and milk; while vegetables and fruit mean vitamins. Yet while we certainly do need protein, it does not have to come from animals, and we do not need as much of it as we might have thought.

Protein, made up of amino acids, is the essential body-building nutrient. Our bodies manufacture all but eight of the amino acids (nine in children) and so these are called the 'essential' amino acids. They exist in animal products (and in soy beans) in roughly the right proportions for human use.

This is how eggs, fish and so on came to be known as sources of 'complete' proteins. This term is obsolete because while meat products may contain 20-per-cent protein, we now know that only about two-thirds of it can actually be used by the body. Today, the buzz-word is 'high-quality' protein. Of animal products, eggs are the top high-quality protein source for humans because they contain all the essential amino acids in the right proportions for our bodies to break down and use.

The way a food provides protein for us is important when considering vegetarianism. Many plant foods are already high in protein – beans, grains, nuts and so on. But when eaten in particular combinations they can give us higher usable protein than dairy or meat products. Eating a mixture of plant foods not only provides variety in color, flavor and texture but also yields a wealth of protein in a form that can be readily metabolized.

'Combinations such as rice and beans, chickpeas and sesame seeds, or peanut butter and wheat bread,' states Gary Null, 'not only provide protein that is more easily absorbed and utilized by the body, but they provide as much protein as animal products.'

The message is that you do not have to rely on meat to provide your protein.

Protein count

How much protein do we need? The World Health Organization (WHO) suggests that 10-15 per cent of your calories (food) should come from protein, and this figure depends on how large you are and what kind of life you lead. Working out precisely what this means in terms of the food you put into your mouth can be complex, but some broad guidelines are found in the **Nutrition Guide** (see p.21) and more detailed information can be found in the galaxy of books on this subject, some of which are listed on p.174. At a basic level, most people in the West, vegetarians included, do not need to worry about specific protein intake because they normally consume plenty of food. And from this you will most probably be ingesting plenty of protein, in the patterns your body can make best use of – from wholewheat bread, peas and beans, nuts, and from cheese and milk.

But it is worth knowing that we do not require protein in the amounts often consumed by regular meat-eaters. And what they may not know is that eating a lot of protein can speed the ageing process, just as it hurries cows and chickens to maturity down on the factory farm. In addition protein

Supermarket saturation: animal fat in meat and dairy products not only makes you flabby, it builds up as cholesterol which is linked to heart disease. Many processed foods like cookies, snacks and desserts are high in saturated fats.

metabolism results in the by-product, urea, which is filtered through the kidneys. Too much going through the system causes strain on these organs.

Meat makes you...unhealthy?

Because it is accompanied by fat, animal protein is also high in calories, leading to overweight in people who eat a lot of it. One 16-ounce steak contains about 1,500 calories – that's about half the average total daily requirement for a grown male. The steak was probably only one element of one meal, and so over-eating is likely – leading to illness and worse. Every year, according to the World Health Organization, around 2.5 million people in the rich world die from heart disease and illnesses associated with obesity.

Sadly, that is not all. The fat in animal products (cheese and milk included) not only fattens you instantaneously, but is high in saturated fat – the type that builds up in your arteries as cholesterol, which in turn is thought to be a major link with heart disease. Our bodies do need fat (or oil rather), but only in small quantities and this should be mono-unsaturated

(olive oil) and poly-unsaturated (safflower, soya) types.

There's another point: our bodies may not be best adapted for digesting meat. The human intestine, 22 feet long, is more suited to vegetarian eating. 'Most carnivores have short intestines,' points out Gary Null. 'But in humans, meat remains in the body for three to four days and putrefies in our blood heat. This putrefication sends toxins through the body and may be one of the major causes of colon and prostate gland problems.'

In addition, there is the fact that where you have meat, you have bacteria. Meat and other animal products are host to the bugs that cause food poisoning. Take salmonella. According to Dr Scott Holmberg of the US Center for Disease Control this form of poisoning hits 'two to four million humans each year, and one of every thousand will die.' Many people do not realize that their diarrhea and vomiting is from contaminated animal products.

Passing on down the digestive tract, as it were, we come to fiber. There is none in meat. No matter how stringy that piece of meat seems, it contains none of the vital bulky material our

Hooked on factory farming: Western intensive meat production is increasing in the Third World. But as cereal-fed meat becomes available for the wealthy minority, the poorest people will have to compete with chickens and cows for grain.

bodies need to scrub the intestinal walls and stimulate the movement of food through the gut.

Potatoes, peas… and a chop

It is plain that we do not need meat for nutrition or for health and that in fact it can harm us to eat it. However, many people are accustomed to it and like the taste. It forms the central part of our meals and has become a symbol of well-being and affluence the world over. So central is it that the food industry has attempted to accommodate vegetarians by producing meat substitutes such as Textured Vegetable Protein (TVP) rather than encouraging people to think in a different way about what goes on a plate. Peter Singer, in *Animal Liberation*, gives an amusing account of an exchange he had with a meat-eater: 'It was clear from the way the questioner phrased his point that he had mentally subtracted his chop from his plate and

was left with a pile of mashed potato and peas.' The person could not conceive of a 'real' meal without meat.

For vegetarians, this probably seems laughable. They know the wealth of the plant world, and enjoy experimenting with the colours, textures and tastes on offer. But perhaps even they will admit that it takes time to adjust to getting the best out of the variety on offer. For many people, conscience-stricken but maybe short on time and ideas for this particular area of their lives, a gradual approach would be to cut down on meat while retaining dairy products in their diet.

Roll over, Beefburger

Purchasing only organic meat, free-range chickens and eggs (even though these cost more) is a way of resisting the powerful meat industry with its hormones and hard-sell. And make no mistake, it is a formidable force. When former US

President Jimmy Carter gave a meatless dinner at the White House in 1977, the President of the American National Cattlemen's Association was hot on the wire, saying that 'The last thing we need is the President of the United States advocating a vegetarian diet for Americans'.

Today, however, millions of people are turning away from meat-eating: over three million Britons are vegetarians (seven per cent of the population), and more than seven million people in the United States. Others are cutting down on meat – 43 per cent of the population in the UK, according to a Gallup Poll survey.

Ironically, among the middle classes in the Third World, regular meat-eating is on the increase as people strive to identify with perceived Western status symbols. Even in India, things are changing. Meat is now seen as a 'virile' food and is being eaten more widely by Hindus. And in its wake comes the ill-health common in the West. 'We are already storing up a time bomb in Africa,' comments Professor Philip James of the UK Rowett Research Institute, 'Cases of high blood pressure in West and South Africa are now increasing at a terrifying rate.'

But the place to start is in our own homes and in those of our relatives and friends. Through our diets we can contribute to change by reducing our impact on the world. So, if we decide we want to, how can we go about helping ourselves and others eat less or no meat?

If you believe that killing animals for food is wrong, then becoming a vegetarian may be easy for you. According to the UK Vegetarian Society, this is a major reason cited by the bulk of new converts, the 11-18 year olds.

You may believe that it is acceptable to eat animal products but still dislike factory-farming methods. In this case, use your power as a consumer to buy only free-range poultry and eggs and organic meat. However you should know that 'free-range' can be a free-ranging term. Often it simply means that the birds are not cooped up in cages roughly the size of this double-page (as they are in 'battery' egg production units). But free-range poultry still live constrained, shortened lives, crowded into dark barns and allowed to do little but eat.

There is 'free-range' meat – but also with a catch as US consumers are finding out. Ranchers have responded to the demands for cattle roaming freely, but lands in 11 states are now overstocked. Thousands of steers, home on the range, are trampling the life out of the soil. One tenth of all US land, most of it in the West, is now becoming eroded and desiccating into desert.

Organic meat usually means that the animal was not treated with drugs or growth hormones. It might also mean that the animals have not been fed the re-hashed remains of other animals, as has been the case in the UK with cattle. These natural herbivores were given dead sheep and chickens, reconstituted as cow cakes to chew over. Sadly some of the sheep's brains carried the infection scrapie, which in cattle developed into Bovine Spongiform Encephalopathy (BSE) or 'mad cow disease'. As far as we know, no humans have yet been infected from eating contaminated beef but in the first months of 1992 the rate of disease in cattle increased from 400 or so cases a week to around 600.

Organic milk or cheese commonly means that the dairy cow grazed on grass that has not been sprayed with chemical weedkillers.

'Somewhere between a shrimp and an oyster'

Cosmetic as these changes may seem if you believe it is wrong to eat animals at all, they are a start – a way for someone who wants to begin the process of reducing the demand for force-fed livestock, fattened for overconsuming Westerners on food that could help feed hungrier people. Where precisely to draw the line between creatures that suffer pain and those that don't is tricky. Somewhere between a shrimp and an oyster is Peter Singer's suggestion.

For other people, health concerns might be uppermost. Knowing that you do not need meat to supply protein and that the flesh is quite bad for you (never mind the chemical additives) is enough. You may find that your desire to eat it slips away.

Once you cut out red meat and veal you can find a label for yourself from the array of vegetarian types listed here:

○ Demi-vegetarians – refuse red meat but still eat fish and poultry as well as dairy produce.
○ Lacto-ovo-vegetarians – eat dairy products and eggs but no meat or fish.
○ Lacto-vegetarians – accept dairy items but exclude eggs.
○ Vegans – do not eat any animal products, even honey.

Despite all the talk and even the acceptance that you do not need meat, it can be hard to forgo a lifelong habit. Taste, custom and culture are the most solid and enduring reasons. Taste at least can be altered: many children, for instance, lose

Jørgen Schytte

Happy eater, Zimbabwe: less meat-eating in the West means more food can be available for others.

ent kinds of meat and poultry, there are over 40 commonly eaten vegetables; 24 kinds of peas, beans and lentils; 20 common fruits; 12 different nuts and nine grains. Although a novice compared to many vegetarians, I now have a wider range of foods on the kitchen shelves. I don't feel as daunted as I used to when walking into whole food stores to confront the packets of fascinating looking 'exotic' beans or lentils.

In part this is because some of these are now more widespread anyway and can be bought in supermarkets. It's a familiarity that has also been helped by the rise of 'ethnic' restaurants and the delicatessen or specialty foodstore – so that we know about garbanzos/chickpeas for instance, through the Middle Eastern *hummus* dip, and want to try making it at home.

Travel is another way some people come across new foods. Certainly, *frijoles refritos* (beans) eaten night after night when I was a penniless traveller in Mexico made their mark as did the myriad corn/maize treats like *quesadillas*. In Africa I fell for *muhogo*, a creamy combination of cassava/manioc and coconut milk. And in Malaysia I warmed to the sizzle and zest of the stir-fries. I can't say I missed meat in any of them and I have made them easily at home.

Testing the recipes for this book has been fun. Most of them are very easy to make and have been adapted for Western kitchens, with substitutes given for any ingredient that may be hard to obtain.

What came across to me, as with the first **NI Food Book**, was the wealth of good everyday food that is eaten around the world. Clearly people everywhere know what is wholesome and tasty. Making sure that they have the means to continue to grow and eat this food is vital. In reducing or ending our meat-eating we can demonstrate that we know our intensive meat production is unsustainable and should not spread to developing countries. If we want to do something in our personal lives to try and end world hunger, then moving to a vegetarian diet is an obvious step.

And it is a pleasure too. I've enjoyed finding out about the variety of plant foods. I've done things with lentils I didn't know could be done and was delighted that the recipe for *dhansak* that I tried really tasted like what I had eaten in an Indian restaurant.

And at the end of a hard day's recipe-testing, with the mountains of dishes to be washed looming by the sink, I found the rum punches from Sri Lanka and the Caribbean particularly refreshing ∎

their sweet tooth as they become adults. For a web of reasons, people eat meat the world over saying 'It's the way we do things. What's wrong with it? We need it'. But people can change.

Food, glorious (vegetarian) food

'On an intellectual level many people are willing to admit that the case for vegetarianism is strong,' comments Peter Singer in *Animal Liberation*. 'Too often, though, there is a gap between intellectual conviction and the action needed to break a lifetime habit.' That strikes a chord with me: I still eat some meat. But finding out more about the impact that this has on world food provision, on animals, and on the environment has made me less inclined to eat it.

By moving meat off my plate I have made more space for the range of other foods. While there are basically five differ-

GUIDE TO NUTRITION

Father feeding child with noodles, China. *Photo: Henry Tse/Tony Stone Worldwide.*

GUIDE TO NUTRITION

*'I submit that scientists have not yet explored the hidden
possibilities of the innumerable seeds, leaves and fruits for
giving the fullest possible nutrition to (humanity).'*
Mahatma Gandhi 1944

THIS is a basic guide to what your body needs and how to find that in non-meat foods. Buy fresh vegetables and fruit and eat them as soon as you can. Green leafy vegetables are a major source of many vitamins and minerals – try and eat them uncooked where appropriate. If you base your meals on salads, vegetables and whole cereals with moderate amounts of nuts, pulses, fruit, dried fruit and dairy products you will obtain all the nutrients you need.

What humans need

Our bodies need water, carbohydrates, fiber, protein, fat, vitamins and minerals. Carbohydrates, protein and fat are known as macronutrients – our requirements for these are measured in milligrams (mg). Equally important, but needed in far smaller amounts are the micronutrients – vitamins, minerals and trace elements – which are measured in micrograms (ug or mcg). In addition to these we need water and fiber.

Regular intakes of nutrients are necessary to maintain our bodies and to give us energy, measured in calories. People's calorie requirement varies according to their age, health, size and activity level. So a small woman with a sedentary life may require 2,000 calories a day while a manual-working man may need 3,500. The World Health Organization's recommended minimum daily intake for adults is 2,600 calories per person, with variations as noted above about your size and lifestyle.

To best nourish the body, these calories should be drawn from the range of nutrients listed above. For although you could rapidly get nearly all the calories you need in a day from eating a pack of butter – half a pound (225g) would yield around 2,025 calories – this would leave your body lacking other vital ingredients.

The main or macro-nutrients (carbohydrates, protein and fat) provide different amounts of calories. Fat, as we have just seen, is very high in calories: one gram of oil, butter or margarine brings nine calories. Carbohydrates (from sugars and starches) provide four calories for each gram, and so does protein (from beans, nuts and dairy foods). Alcohol brings seven calories per gram (or milliliter), so a glass of dry white wine would be about 100 calories.

PROTEIN

This makes up part of the structure of every cell in our bodies, and since cells are constantly dying and being replaced we require a steady supply of protein for this rebuilding. Infants and children need plenty as they are growing rapidly.

Proteins are made up of amino acids containing molecules of carbon, hydrogen, nitrogen, oxygen and sulphur. There are around 20 amino acids altogether and all life forms have them. Humans can synthesize (manufacture) some of the amino acids from other foods, but there are eight (nine in children) which must be ingested. These are the 'essential' amino acids – valine, leucine, isoleucine, lysine, threonine, tryptophan, methionine, phenylalanine (and histadine for children).

Foods contain amino acids in differing proportions. The highest-quality protein foods contain the most complete set of essential amino acids in the right proportions for the body to be able to make the best use of them. Apart from soy beans, single plant foods do not contain all the essential amino acids in the right proportions. However when we mix foods in our meals any lack in one can be offset by another – for example, pulses are low in methionine but rich in lysine,

The protein grams in various foods

	grams of protein
2 ounces / 60 g of milk in tea or coffee	2.0
4 ounces / 110 g cheddar cheese	31.0
3 1/2 ounces / 100 g low fat cottage cheese	13.8
3 1/2 ounces / 100 g very low fat cottage cheese	11.9
1 1/2 ounces / 50 g (1 serving) muesli	5.1
5 1/4 ounces / 150 g plain yogurt	7.5
1 1/4 cups / 300 ml / 1/2 pint skimmed or soy milk	10.0
1 egg	7.0
2 ounces / 60 g (1 serving) Shredded Wheat	5.0
2 slices wholemeal bread	6.0
1 cup / 150 g whole wheat spaghetti	21.0
8 ounces / 225 g baked potato	6.0
1 small tin baked beans	8.0
5 ounces / 150 g bean-curd/tofu	16.0
3 1/2 ounces / 100 g soy flour	36.8
2 ounces / 60 g lentils, haricot or butter beans	10.0
1 cup / 150 g peanuts	36.0
3/4-ounce / 20-g serving peanut butter	4.8
2 ounces / 60 g almonds, cashews, sesame seeds or sunflower seeds	10.0
1 cup / 100 g dried apricots	4.8
1/2 cup / 100 g spinach (cooked)	5.1
3 1/2 ounces / 100 g avocado pear	4.2

The World Health Organization recommends that around 10 per cent of a person's energy intake should be in the form of protein. So on an intake of 2,600 calories (WHO's recommended daily minimum for adults) about 260 should be as protein. Since each gram of protein provides four calories, you would therefore need 65 g of protein each day, depending on your age, sex, lifestyle and so on. The WHO figure leaves a comfortable margin: the UK Vegetarian Society suggests that 45 g per day for women and 55.5 g for men is plenty.

People in the rich world rarely lack protein – overall we consume well over the necessary amount of calories – US 3,666; Aotearoa/New Zealand 3,459; Canada 3,447; Australia 3,322; UK 3,252 – and within that food there is likely to be sufficient protein. But we consume a lot of energy as fat and sugar, often resulting in heart disease and illnesses associated with obesity which kill around 2.5 million people each year.

We have an abundance of protein-rich foods readily available all year round. Vegetarian foods rich in protein are nuts, seeds, pulses (peas, beans, lentils), grains, soy products, dairy produce and eggs (see box left). And of course, other foods you eat such as vegetables, salads and fruit contribute small amounts of amino acids as well.

CARBOHYDRATES

Although protein and fat also provide calories, it is the carbohydrates which are our main source of energy. These normally come from plant foods in the form of sugars and starches.

Where possible, avoid sugars and refined starches such as white bread or flour and white rice as although they bring calories, these are 'empty' – they bring few nutrients to the body. On a diet high in refined starches and sugar people quickly become unhealthy because they lack vitamins and minerals. By contrast, cereals such as wholemeal bread, pasta and oats; and root vegetables like potatoes and parsnips bring nourishment to your body for the same amount of calories. They also provide fiber or roughage, the indigestible but essential material which keeps food moving regularly along the gut (see box below).

while cereals are the other way about. Eaten together as beans on toast, cereal with milk or rice and peas the amino acids complement each other and you get well-balanced protein.

Many 'traditional' diets in the South are made up of these complementing ingredients – lentils and rice in India; hummus (chickpeas and sesame seed paste) with wheat pitta bread in the Middle East and beans with corn/maize tortillas in Latin America. Adding dairy produce and eggs also supplies missing amino acids, and as your body can store them for short periods it is unlikely that you would go short.

Some sources of fiber

Almonds ● Bran ● Brazil nuts ● Dates ● Dried apricots ● Dried/desiccated coconut ● Dried figs ● Haricot beans ● Oatmeal ● Parsley ● Peanuts ● Prunes ● Raspberries ● Soy flour ● Wholewheat flour/bread

Grams of fat per 3¹/₂ ounces / 100g of selected foods

	grams of fat
Almonds	53.5
Avocado pear	22.2
Brown rice	0.6
Butter beans	0.3
Lentils/kidney beans	0.5
Peanuts	49.0
Soy flour	23.5
Butter/margarine	82.0
Camembert	23.0
Cheddar	33.5
Cottage cheese, low fat	3.9
Cottage cheese, very low fat	1.9
Oil	100.0
Yogurt, plain	1.1
Chocolate digestive biscuits/cookies	24.0
Ice-cream	8.2
Chocolate	36.75
Crisps/chips	35.0
Mayonnaise	42.0

FATS AND OILS

We all need a little fat to keep body tissues healthy, for the manufacture of hormones and to carry the vitamins A, D, E and K. Fats are made up of smaller components called fatty acids. Two of these, linoleic and linolenic, are essential for humans and they are widely found in plant foods.

There are saturated and unsaturated fats – this refers to how much hydrogen they contain. Saturated fats, found mainly in animal products, contain cholesterol. This is necessary for health but our bodies can produce what they require. Excess cholesterol may build up as deposits on the walls of arteries and clog them, leading to an increased risk of heart disease. Saturated fats raise blood cholesterol levels while unsaturated fats lower them. Mono-unsaturated fats such as olive oil have a neutral effect.

Oils which are high in polyunsaturates (and which contain the two essential fatty acids) are safflower, soy bean oil and sunflower oil. Margarines made of these can also be high in polyunsaturated fat.

In general, people in rich countries eat too much fat and oil, much of it saturated. Very often the fat is hidden in processed foods such as cakes, biscuits, ice-cream, chips and pies. Fat comprises over one-third of a chocolate bar and delicatessen meat products and pâtés have fat added to that already in the meat used. In the West, many people consume about five ounces/120 g of fat a day. Remembering that each gram of fat delivers nine calories, that is 1,080 calories before you start adding in the calories from protein and carbohydrates.

How much fat should you eat? WHO advises between 15-30 per cent of your total energy intake, with no more than 10 per cent of it in the form of saturated fat. So if your total calorie intake is the WHO average of 2,600, and 20 per cent of this comes from fat, that would be 520 calories. Since each gram of fat brings nine calories, this means you should eat about 58 g or two ounces a day. Many of the fast foods eaten today, especially by children and fat adults, contain high amounts of fat. In French fries/chips for example, 50 per cent of the calories are from fat; in a pork sausage, 65 per cent; while in a packet of crisps/chips it accounts for 60 per cent of the total energy.

Meat contributes over 25 per cent of all fat in meat-eaters' diets so cutting out meat or reducing your consumption of it will be a help. Dairy products are also saturated fat-laden, especially hard cheeses, cream and whole milk – but you are unlikely to polish off half a pound of cheese at one go, whereas an 8-ounce steak could quickly disappear.

There are plenty of dairy products which are low fat, so they deliver the useful protein without the potential for flab. Yogurt, cottage and other low-fat cheeses and skimmed milk are all available in supermarkets.

Plant foods rich in fats – avocado pears, nuts and seeds – should also be eaten in moderation, ideally in their raw state, and as part of a meal rather than as a snack. However unlike crisps or French fries, nuts and seeds provide protein, vitamins and a substantial amount of fiber. Pulses, whole grains, vegetables and fruit are low in fat.

In addition to the main or macro-nutrients – protein, carbohydrates and fats – our bodies need vitamins, minerals and trace elements (the micro-nutrients).

VITAMINS

This is the name for a group of unrelated nutrients that the body cannot synthesize for itself either at all or in sufficient quantities. Only small amounts are needed but they must be included in our food. Vitamins are essential for growth, cell repair and regulating metabolism (the rate at which the body consumes energy).

Vitamin A (retinol)

This is essential for healthy eyes and skin and for seeing in dim light. Lack of vitamin A leads to low resistance to infection, skin complaints, fatigue and night blindness.

It is found in animal products but our bodies can also manufacture it from carotene which occurs in red and yellow vegetables such as carrots, tomatoes, apricots and bell peppers as well as in green vegetables. It is usually added to margarine.

Some sources of Vitamin A

Broccoli ● Carrots ● Cheddar ● Dandelion leaves ● Dried apricots ● Eggs ● Mangoes ● Melon ● Milk ● Parsley ● Sorrel ● Spinach ● Sweet potatoes ● Watercress

Vitamin B_1 (thiamin)

Thiamin converts carbohydrates into energy and is essential for growth and health of skin, nerves and muscles. It is easily destroyed through cooking and storage.

Deficiency of thiamin leads to depression and nervous disorders; poor digestion, skin and hair.

Some sources of Vitamin B_1

Bran ● Brazil nuts ● Hazelnuts ● Millet ● Oatmeal ● Peanuts ● Peas ● Rye flour ● Soy flour ● Walnuts ● Wheatgerm ● Wholewheat flour/bread ● Yeast extract

Vitamin B_2 (riboflavin)

Vitamin B_2 is important for growth and for healthy skin, mouth and eyes. It is destroyed by light. Milk, a main source, can lose up to 70 per cent of B_2 content if it is left in sunlight for two hours.

Lack of B_2 shows as bloodshot eyes, mouth sores, dry hair and skin, nervousness and tiredness.

Some sources of Vitamin B_2

Almonds ● Brie, Cheddar and other cheeses ● Broccoli ● Broad beans ● Dates ● Dried peaches ● Eggs ● Milk ● Millet ● Mushrooms ● Soy flour and products ● Wheatgerm ● Wholewheat bread ● Yogurt

Vitamin B_3 (niacin or nicotinic acid)

This is essential for growth, for healthy skin and nerves as well as for the digestion of carbohydrates. Deficiency of this vitamin can result in irritability, nervousness, stomach upsets, headaches and insomnia. Severe lack causes pellagra, a skin disease. The vitamin can be produced in the body from the amino acid tryptophan, found in milk and eggs.

Some sources of Vitamin B_3

Bran ● Broad beans ● Dates ● Dried apricots ● Dried peaches ● Millet ● Mushrooms ● Peanuts ● Soy flour ● Wholewheat flour/bread ● Yeast extract

Vitamin B_6 (pyridoxine)

B_6 is essential for the body's use of protein; for health of skin, nerves and muscles. It is particularly important for women who are pregnant, who use the contraceptive pill, or who suffer from pre-menstrual tension. High alcohol consumption increases the body's need for this vitamin, and it is most effective in conjunction with vitamin B_2 and magnesium. B_6 is easily destroyed by cooking. Lack of it brings irritability, depression, skin complaints, insomnia, fatigue, anemia and migraine.

Some sources of Vitamin B_6

Avocado pear ● Bananas ● Bran ● Brie and other cheeses ● Brussels sprouts ● Cauliflower ● Currants, sultanas ● Hazelnuts ● Milk ● Peanuts ● Prunes ● Rye flour ● Soy flour ● Walnuts ● Wheatgerm ● Wholewheat flour/bread ● Yeast extract

Vitamin B_{12} (cobalmins or cyanocobalamin)

This is required for growth and for the body's use of protein as well as for health of nerves and skin. It is easily destroyed by light and heat.

Deficiency leads to anemia, tiredness, skin disorders and in extreme cases, paralysis. B_{12} is mainly found in animal prod-

Salt production in Sri Lanka. *Photo: Mark Edwards/Still Pictures.*

ucts and if you are a vegan you need to take a supplement of this vitamin or eat products which have been fortified with it.

Some sources of Vitamin B_{12}
Cheese • Cottage cheese • Cream • Eggs • Milk • Yeast extract • Yogurt

Folic acid (B group)

Folic acid is vital for growth, fertility and healthy blood. As its name suggests, it is found in leafy vegetables. The vitamin is easily lost in cooking so eat plenty of raw salad leaves. In particular, pregnant women and those taking oral contraceptives need folic acid.

Deficiency results in anemia, depression, diarrhea, and fetal neural tube defects.

Some sources of Folic acid
Almonds • Avocado pear • Bran • Broccoli • Cabbage • Hazelnuts • Parsley • Peanuts • Peas • Spinach • Sweet potatoes • Yeast extract

Biotin and pantothenic acid (B group)

Biotin is essential for good skin, nerves and muscles and its lack can lead to hair loss and eczema. Pantothenic acid promotes hair and other tissue growth, and deficiency gives dry skin and hair.

These vitamins are found in eggs, yeast, wheatgerm, nuts, wholemeal bread and brown rice.

Vitamin C (ascorbic acid)

This maintains connective tissue between cells; it is needed for health of teeth and gums; for proper absorption of iron (best eaten at the same meal); it helps prevent disease and aids recovery. Larger amounts are needed by people under stress or

Some sources of Vitamin C
Bell peppers, red and green • Blackcurrants • Broccoli • Cabbage • Grapefruit • Lemons • Lychees • Mangoes • Oranges • Parsley • Radishes • Raspberries • Sorrel • Spinach • Strawberries • Watercress

taking drugs including antibiotics, tranquillizers, alcohol, nicotine and coffee. Vitamin C is destroyed by cooking and heat. To avoid deficiency, eat plenty of raw fruit and vegetables, and only lightly cook the rest.

Deficiency leads to weakening of connective tissue and bleeding (of gums), as well as low resistance to infection.

Vitamin D (calciferol)

This is required for the absorption of calcium and phosphorus, and in the formation of bones and teeth. It is formed by the action of sunlight on oils in the skin and it is also available in dairy and other foods. Lack of vitamin D can lead to rickets, and to weakened or porous bones.

Some sources of Vitamin D
Butter • Cheese • Eggs • Margarine • Sunlight

Vitamin E (tocopherol)

This is needed for body cell formation and maintenance and possibly for fertility. It also helps wounds heal without scarring and may have a rejuvenating effect.

It is rare to have a deficiency of this vitamin, but it causes tiredness and anemia. Vitamin E is available in most foods.

Vitamin K

Vitamin K is essential for blood-clotting. Lack of it leads to prolonged bleeding, but deficiency is rare since it occurs widely in vegetables and cereals.

MINERALS

These are required, like vitamins, to keep the body functioning properly. Calcium, iron, potassium and magnesium are the main minerals and the others such as zinc and iodine are known as trace elements and are needed only in tiny amounts.

Calcium

This is vital for healthy bones, teeth and nerves, and vitamin

cont/d on page 30

Some sources of Calcium
Almonds • Brazil nuts • Brie • Camembert • Cheddar and similar cheeses • Dried figs • Eggs • Milk • Parmesan • Parsley • Sesame seeds • Soy flour • Spinach • Watercress • Yogurt

Food facts – at a glance

Knowing the nutritional make-up of some of the most common vegetarian foods can help you to eat a balanced and healthy diet. Below, foods are listed with their protein, carbohydrate, fiber and fat content given as the number of grams contained in each 3$\frac{1}{2}$ ounces / 100 grams of that food. Where foods contain significant amounts of vitamins and minerals, these are listed.

Key: **Fo** folic acid   **Fe** iron   **Ca** calcium
Na sodium   **K** potassium   **Mg** magnesium
P phosphorus   **Zn** zinc   **T** trace only   **–** no data.
Vitamins are listed before the semi-colon; minerals after.

BEANS, LENTILS

	Protein	Carbohydrate	Fiber	Fat	Calories	Vitamins/Minerals
Kidney beans	7.8	21.4	–	0.5	118	B_1 B_2 B_3 B_6 B_{12}; Fe
Mung beans	22.0	35.6	–	1.0	231	B_1; Fe P K
Lentils	7.6	17.0	3.7	0.5	99	B_6; Fe
Broad beans	4.1	7.1	4.2	0.6	48	B_3
Butter beans	7.1	17.1	5.1	0.3	95	K Zn
Haricot beans	6.6	16.6	7.4	0.5	93	Fe Mg Zn
Soy flour	36.8	23.5	11.9	23.5	447	B_1 B_2 B_3 B_6; Ca Fe K Mg P

NUTS

	Protein	Carbohydrate	Fiber	Fat	Calories	Vitamins/Minerals
Almonds	16.9	4.3	14.3	53.5	565	B_1 B_2 B_3 Fo E; Ca Fe K Mg P Zn
Brazils	12.0	4.1	9.0	61.5	619	B_1 B_3 B_6 E; Ca Fe K Mg P Zn
Hazelnuts	7.6	6.8	6.1	36.0	380	B_1 B_6 Fo E; Mg P Zn
Peanuts (raw)	24.3	8.6	8.1	49.0	570	B_1 B_3 B_6 Fo E; K Mg P Zn
Walnuts	10.6	5.0	5.2	51.5	525	B_1 B_3 B_6 Fo; Fe K Mg P Zn
Peanut butter	22.6	13.1	7.6	53.7	623	B_1 B_3 B_6 Fo E; K Mg Na P Zn

VEGETABLES

	Protein	Carbohydrate	Fiber	Fat	Calories	Vitamins/Minerals
Avocado pear	4.2	1.8	2.0	22.2	223	B_6 Fo E
Broccoli (cooked)	3.1	1.6	4.1	T	18	A B_2 Fo C
Cabbage (raw)	3.3	3.3	3.1	T	26	A B_6 Fo C
Carrots (raw)	0.7	5.4	2.9	T	23	A B_6; Na
Cauliflower	1.6	0.8	1.8	T	9	B_3 Fo C
Courgettes/zucchini (cooked)	1.0	2.5	0.6	0.1	12	
Cucumber	0.6	1.8	0.4	0.1	10	
Lettuce	1.0	1.2	1.5	0.4	12	A Fo
Mushrooms	1.8	0.0	2.5	0.6	13	B_2 B_3 Fo; K
Onions	0.9	5.2	1.3	T	23	
Parsley	5.2	T	9.1	T	21	A B_2 B_6 C; Ca Fe K
Peas (cooked)	5.0	7.7	5.2	0.4	52	A B_1 B_3 Fo
Green bell pepper	0.9	2.2	0.9	0.4	15	A B_6 C
Potatoes (baked)	2.6	25.0	2.5	0.1	105	B_3 B_6
Potatoes (boiled)	1.4	19.7	1.0	0.1	80	B_6
Spinach (cooked)	5.1	1.4	6.3	0.5	30	A B_2 B_6 Fo C E; Ca Fe Na K Mg
Sweet potatoes (cooked)	1.1	20.1	2.3	0.6	85	A B_6 Fo E
Tomatoes	0.9	2.8	1.5	T	14	Fo C
Watercress	2.9	0.7	3.3	T	14	A Fo C; Ca Na

DAIRY PRODUCTS

	Protein	Carbohydrate	Fiber	Fat	Calories	Vitamins/ Minerals
Cheese: cheddar types	26.0	T	–	33.5	406	A B_2 B_{12} Fo D; Ca Na P Zn
Cheese: brie types	22.8	T	–	23.2	300	A B_2 B_6 B_{12} Fo D; Ca Na P Zn
Cottage cheese	11.9	3.3	–	1.9	78	B_2 B_{12} Ca Na P
Eggs	12.3	T	–	10.9	147	A B_2 B_{12} Fo D E; Na
Cows' milk – whole	3.3	4.7	–	3.8	65	A B_2 B_{12}; Ca
Cows' milk – skimmed	3.4	5.0	–	0.1	33	B_2 B_{12}; Ca
Goats' milk	3.3	4.6	–	4.5	71	A B_2; Ca
Yogurt	5.0	6.2	–	1.0	52	B_2; Ca

DRIED FRUIT

	Protein	Carbohydrate	Fiber	Fat	Calories	Vitamins/ Minerals
Apricots	4.8	43.4	24.0	T	182	A B_2 B_3 B_6; Ca Fe Na K Mg
Dates	2.0	63.9	8.7	T	248	B_3 B_6 Fo; Mg
Figs	3.6	52.9	18.5	T	213	B_3 B_6; Ca Fe Na K Mg
Peaches	3.4	53.0	14.3	T	212	A B_2 B_3; Fe K
Prunes	2.4	40.3	16.1	T	161	A B_2 B_3 B_6; K
Raisins	1.1	64.4	6.8	T	246	B_6; Na K Mg
Sultanas	1.8	64.7	7.0	T	250	B_6; Na K

FRESH FRUIT

	Protein	Carbohydrate	Fiber	Fat	Calories	Vitamins/ Minerals
Apples	0.3	11.9	2.0	T	46	
Bananas	1.1	19.2	3.4	0.3	79	B_6 Fo
Cherries	0.6	11.9	1.7	T	47	
Figs	1.3	9.5	2.5	T	41	A
Black grapes	0.6	15.5	0.4	T	61	
Grapefruit	0.6	5.3	0.6	T	22	C
Lemons	0.8	3.2	5.2	T	15	C; Ca
Mangoes	0.5	15.3	1.5	T	59	A C
Oranges	0.8	8.5	2.0	T	35	C Fo
Peaches	0.6	9.1	1.4	T	37	A B_3
Pears	0.3	10.6	2.3	T	41	
Pineapple	0.5	11.6	1.2	T	46	C
Strawberries	0.6	6.2	2.2	T	26	Fo C

GRAINS

	Protein	Carbohydrate	Fiber	Fat	Calories	Vitamins/ Minerals
Bran	14.1	26.8	44.0	5.5	206	B_1 B_2 B_3 B_6 Fo E; Ca Fe K Mg P Zn
Wholewheat bread	8.8	41.8	8.5	2.7	216	B_1 B_3 Fo; Fe Na Mg P Zn
Wholewheat flour	13.2	65.8	9.6	2.0	318	B_1 B_3 B_6 Fo E; Fe Mg P Zn
Millet	9.9	72.9	3.2	2.9	327	B_1 B_2 B_3; Fe K Mg P
Oatmeal	12.4	72.8	7.0	8.7	401	B_1 B_3 Fo; Fe Mg P Zn
Brown rice	2.5	25.5	0.3	0.6	119	B_3; Na
Wheatgerm	26.5	44.7	–	8.1	347	B_1 B_2 B_3 B_6 Fo E; Fe K Mg P

D must be present for its proper absorption. Lack of calcium can result in nervous exhaustion, insomnia and cramps. Pregnant and breastfeeding women and those on the contraceptive pill, cortisone and steroid drugs have a particular need.

Iron

This mineral carries oxygen around the body and also plays a part in the formation of red blood cells. Its absorption is enhanced by vitamin C eaten at the same meal. Lack of iron leads to anemia, fatigue, poor memory.

Some sources of Iron

Almonds ● Baked (haricot) beans ● Bran ● Brazil nuts ● Cashew nuts ● Chickpeas/garbanzos ● Cocoa ● Curry powder ● Dried apricots, figs, peaches, prunes, raisins ● Eggs ● Hazelnuts ● Lentils ● Millet ● Molasses ● Oatmeal and whole grains ● Parsley ● Pumpkin, sesame and sunflower seeds ● Soy beans ● Soy flour ● Spinach ● Yeast extract

Sodium and potassium

These are the minerals which control the body's water balance. Sodium (salt) is commonly eaten to excess in Western diets and this condition is linked to kidney disorders and high blood pressure with its risks of strokes and heart attacks. Too much sodium inhibits the absorption of potassium.

Lack of potassium can lead to heart attacks. Potassium is found in many foods but can easily be destroyed when vegetables are overcooked. Deficiency can occur when little raw food is eaten and the diet is high in refined foods and salt.

Some sources of Potassium

Almonds ● Bran ● Brazil nuts ● Dried apricots ● Dried figs ● Dried peaches ● Molasses ● Parsley ● Prunes ● Raisins ● Soy flour ● Sultanas ● Yeast extract

Magnesium

Needed to retain potassium in the cells, magnesium also aids the proper functioning of vitamin B_6.

Lack of it leads to muscle cramps, nervous depression and convulsions, but deficiency is rare.

Phosphorus

Essential for bones and teeth, this mineral is involved in the

Some sources of Magnesium

Almonds ● Bran ● Brazil nuts ● Chickpeas/garbanzos ● Dried apricots ● Haricot beans ● Millet ● Oatmeal ● Peanuts ● Soy flour ● Walnuts ● Spinach ● Wheatgerm ● Wholewheat flour/bread

use of B vitamins. It is found in many foods, especially those which are good sources of calcium.

Zinc

This is present in many foods but it is not always readily absorbed. Although its exact role is not completely defined, deficiency can result in stunted growth, infertility and slow healing of wounds.

Low zinc levels are found in people with high blood pressure, women who are pregnant or on contraceptive pills, and heavy drinkers.

Some sources of Zinc

Almonds ● Bran ● Brazil nuts ● Brie and similar cheeses ● Cheddar and similar cheeses ● Hazelnuts ● Oatmeal ● Parmesan ● Rye flour ● Walnuts ● Wholewheat flour/bread

Iodine

Non-vegetarians can obtain iodine from fish. It is also found in dairy products, and in vegetables but here the amount will depend on how much iodine was present in the soil where the vegetables grew.

Iodine is an essential part of some hormones and deficiency can lead to thyroid gland disease, a high blood cholesterol level and also affects mental and physical functioning.

Some sources of Iodine

Cheese ● Eggs ● Milk ● Nuts ● Olive oil ● Onions ● Seaweed ● Watercress ● Wholemeal bread ● Yogurt

There are many other minerals needed in only tiny amounts and these will be ingested when you eat other foods. In general you do not need to worry about the quantity of vitamins and minerals unless you are on a strict diet for medical reasons ■

NOTES TO THE RECIPES

Woman winnowing millet grain, Mali. *Photo: Mark Edwards/Still Pictures.*

NOTES TO THE RECIPES

(see also **Nutrition Guide**, p.21 and **Glossary**, p.163)

MEASURES for salt, fat and sugar in this book are given as guide amounts only: if you want to use less or no sugar, that is up to you. If you prefer to cut out the salt altogether, then go ahead.

The reason this is important is not just because of your health but also because the idea of being flexible about what you put into a pot is a useful, some may say essential, part of cooking – to experiment, to add or take out something. This approach also reflects the way most people cook in the developing world where recipe books are few and far between, and the best cooking goes on at home with hand-me-down favorites.

So while this book gives the measures for the main ingredients required to make each dish, please feel free to experiment.

Beans, peas and lentils (pulses or legumes)

In the recipes, the measures given for these are for the **dry unsoaked, uncooked ingredients**. If you want to use canned beans, check the recipe quantities and cooking

Cooking times for selected pulses

The pulses below need soaking for 8-12 hours (overnight) before cooking, except those marked*.
See also packet instructions.

Bean	Approximate cooking time	In pressure cooker
Azuki beans	45 minutes	15 minutes
Black beans	1 hour	20 minutes
Black-eyed beans/ cowpeas	50 minutes	15 minutes
Borlotti beans	1^1/$_2$ hours	25 minutes
Broad beans	1^1/$_2$ hours	40 minutes
Butter or Lima beans	1^1/$_2$ hours	20 minutes
Cannellini beans	50 minutes	15 minutes
Chickpeas/garbanzos	1^1/$_2$ hours	30 minutes
Flageolet beans	50 minutes	20 minutes
Haricot beans	50 minutes	20 minutes
Mung beans	45 minutes	15 minutes
Mung dal *	30 minutes	–
Pigeon peas/gunga	45 minutes	15 minutes
Toor dal *	30 minutes	–
Pinto beans	50 minutes	15 minutes
Red kidney beans	1 hour	20 minutes
Rosecoco or sugar beans	50 minutes	20 minutes
Soy beans	2^1/$_2$ hours	50 minutes
Whole green peas	1^1/$_2$ hours	30 minutes
Split peas *	45 minutes	–
Whole lentils *	45 minutes	15 minutes
Split lentils *	20 minutes	–
Urad dal *	30 minutes	–

methods. After soaking, dried beans should be boiled rapidly for the first 10 minutes to destroy any toxins before you continue to cook them as normal. Soy beans need to boil hard for the first hour. A basic pressure cooker is very useful for cooking beans more quickly.

Bulghur and cracked wheat

If using bulghur, pour boiling water over it and leave to soak for about 40 minutes, then drain and use. For cracked wheat, boil for 20 minutes and then let it stand in the pan for a few minutes more, or cook these items according to the instructions on the packet.

Cassava/manioc

Cassava/manioc should always be peeled and cooked before eating as it contains substances which can give rise to prussic acid, but this is readily destroyed by cooking. The most common way to cook cassava is to cut it into chunks and then boil it for about 30 minutes, or according to the recipe. You can also buy it as dried granules, *gari*, and this can be made into a porridge.

Chilis, chili powder, curry powder, other spices and herbs

The measures given for these ingredients are **guide amounts** only. If you are not sure how hot you like something, or if the spice or herb is unfamiliar, start by using a little and add more later if you wish. In general, food tastes better if you use fresh spices and herbs.

If the chili is not broken or chopped, and therefore the seeds do not get into the dish, then the chili will not make it hot but will impart a smoky flavor. Discard the chili before serving if desired. If you do not want a chili to be too hot, then cut it longitudinally and take out its seeds.

Coconut milk

You can now often buy this in a canned, creamed or powdered form (see p.125 for how to make these up for use in recipes).

Fat and oil

In general, the recipes do not specify the amount of oil or fat to use. The advice is to use as little as possible to begin with and add further small amounts if necessary. Most recipes call simply for 'margarine' or 'oil'. Here it is best to use varieties high in polyunsaturated fat such as corn, safflower, sunflower or soy bean. If you want to use red palm oil or *dendê*, coconut oil or ghee (clarified butter), remember that these are high in saturated fats and should not be eaten frequently or in large amounts.

However for special occasions you may like to use these ingredients for their characteristic flavor.

You can use a wok for most

deep-frying required in these recipes. Drain fried food on absorbent paper towels where possible.

Remember that there is fat in cheese and in snack foods such as chips and crackers. Many processed foods are made with saturated fats.

Fiber

Fruit, vegetables, pulses or legumes (beans, peas and so on), seeds and whole grains provide different kinds of fiber. Oats, for example, provide soluble fiber which may help reduce cholesterol levels. Where possible, eat brown rice or pasta and wholemeal/wholewheat flour as well as fresh fruit, seeds, legumes and raw or lightly-cooked vegetables.

Flour

Unless specified otherwise, 'flour' in the recipes means wheat flour. You can use wholemeal/wholewheat interchangeably with refined, or use half and half, but bear in mind that wholemeal/wholewheat flour makes a more solid product. It is a good idea to sieve it as this helps aerate it. Just tip the remaining bran in afterwards.

Mixing in some soy flour is a good way to increase the protein content of a dish especially for children: one part soy to three parts of wheat flour is fine for most general uses. If you find wholemeal/wholewheat pastry

difficult to roll out for a pie base, then put the mixture into the pie-dish and press it into place with a metal spoon.

Fruit and vegetables

With concern about fiber on the one hand and anxiety about pesticide residues on the other, it is difficult to advize how to prepare the fruit and vegetables you will be using. Organically-grown produce is obviously the best, if you can obtain it. If not, wash the fruit and vegetables carefully and leave them unpeeled if you can.

In the recipes, it is assumed these items are washed and peeled as desired.

Grains

Unrefined cereals (whole grains) contain the germ which is the source of oils, proteins and minerals. The bran is an important source of fiber. Grains can be bought in

various forms from whole to cracked, and toasted to par-boiled.

The chart gives an idea of preparation and boiling times, but refer also to the packet instructions.

Measures

All measures in the book are in US cups and Metric. Where US and UK spell a word differently, the US version is generally used. Names for ingredients may differ in your country.

While teaspoon measures are the same, British table-spoon measures are larger than in North America and Australasia. UK readers should therefore use only a scant tablespoon amount.

Nuts and seeds

Amounts given for these are for **shelled but raw** (unroasted) items, unless stated otherwise. See also toasting and roasting on next page.

Cooking times for selected grains

Grain	Preparation	Liquid per cup of grain	Approximate cooking time	In pressure cooker
Barley	toast	4 cups	1 hour	20 minutes
Buckwheat	toast or fry	3 cups	20 minutes	8 minutes
Corn/maize	–	4 cups	5-10 minutes	–
Millet	toast or fry	3 cups	20 minutes	8 minutes
Oats	can toast rinse	3 cups	30 minutes	12 minutes
Quinoa	can toast	2 cups	15 minutes	–
Rice (brown)	can toast or fry	2 cups	30 minutes	10 minutes
Wheat berries	soak 12 hours	4 cups	1 hour	10 minutes
Wild rice	–	3 cups	1 hour	20 minutes

Peppers/bell peppers

Where a recipe calls for bell peppers these are the large sweet red or green varieties.

Plantains/green (savory) bananas

These are easier to peel if you boil them first for about 30 minutes. If you have to peel them before cooking, it helps to cut the plantain in half and then make lengthwise cuts in each section in order to remove the peel.

Quinoa

This Andean high-protein grain should be rinsed well before cooking as the seeds are naturally coated with saponin, an acrid and slightly toxic substance. Packaged quinoa is presoaked and scrubbed free of saponin, but it is worth rinsing it again before you cook it.

Stock or water

Use stock if possible as it gives a much better flavor to the dish. Vegetarian stock cubes are available, or make your own stock using either Vegamite/Marmite and/or vegetables.

Sugar and Honey

Where sugar is listed as an ingredient, the measure is given as a **guide amount**. You may prefer to reduce this or even omit it altogether. Remember, brown sugar is just as bad for you as white. Honey can be substituted where appropriate. It contains fewer calories than sugar but that's still too many for most of us, and its tooth-rotting qualities are intact.

Toasting/roasting

To toast grains, nuts and seeds, broil or grill them gently, shaking often. You can also put them in a heavy shallow pan, without oil, and heat them until they go a shade darker (or follow individual recipe instructions).

Store-cupboard

A few items that are handy to keep in stock.
*For details on some less familiar ones see **Glossary**, p.163*

DRIED HERBS AND SPICES

Black pepper
Caraway seeds
Cardamom pods
Chili powder
Cinnamon sticks
  and ground cinnamon
Coriander seeds
  and ground coriander
Cumin seeds
  and ground cumin
Curry powder
Dill
Fenugreek seeds
Garam masala
Ginger root
  and ground ginger
Marjoram
Nutmeg
Paprika
Parsley
Turmeric

DRIED FRUIT, NUTS AND SEEDS

Apricots
Dates
Figs
Raisins
Sultanas
Almonds
Brazil nuts
Cashews
Hazelnuts
Peanuts
Pistachios
Walnuts
Poppy seeds
Pumpkin seeds
Sesame seeds
Sunflower seeds

CANNED FOODS

Corn
Garbanzos/chickpeas

Kidney and other beans
Tomatoes

GRAINS AND PASTA

Brown rice
Buckwheat
Bulghur and/or
  cracked wheat
Corn/maize flour/meal
Millet/flour
Oats
Quinoa
Wholewheat flour
Wholewheat spaghetti and
  other pasta

FRESH HERBS

Cilantro/coriander
Parsley

QUICK-COOKING PULSES

Mung dal
Red lentils

Toor dal
Urad dal
Green split peas
Yellow split peas

MISCELLANEOUS

Chilis
Dried mushrooms
Dried seaweed
Peanut butter
Sesame paste (tahini)
Tomato paste

STARTERS, SNACKS AND SOUPS

Cooking the evening meal, Matlab, Bangladesh. *Photo: Mark Edwards/Still Pictures.*

GHANA

Kosie (Cowpea/black-eyed bean snack)

Makes 15-20

West African food, rich in variety, rests on the staples of rice, yams, cassava/manioc, and plantains or cooking bananas. These are cooked into a porridge and usually served with a sauce or stew made from peanuts/groundnuts, okra/ladies' fingers, and a range of beans and greens spiced up with chilis.

'*Kosie* is a snack food from northern Ghana. It is commonly sold on the streets, often garnished with onions.' *John Haigh, Kumasi, Ghana*

I N G R E D I E N T S

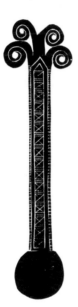

- **1 cup / 225 g cowpeas/black-eyed beans, cooked**
- **¹/₂-1 onion, finely sliced**
- **1 green chili, or 1 teaspoon chili powder**
- **1 egg**
- **oil**
- **water**
- **a few onion rings**
- **salt**

1. First of all, mash the drained beans in a bowl using a fork.

2. Next add the onion and chili and mix well or blend to make a smooth paste.

3. When this is done, put in the egg, a little water and salt and beat for several minutes until the mixture is frothy.

4. In a heavy pan, heat enough oil to shallow-fry and then place spoonfuls of the mixture in to cook for a few minutes, turning once.

5. Drain and serve with sliced onion rings (cooked or raw), chutney or tomato sauce ∎

Kaakro (Plantain/savory banana snack)

Serves 4-6

Plantains or bananas are widely used in Ghanaian cooking and, together with beans, peanuts/groundnuts, rice, fish and guinea fowl supply the basis of the national cuisine. *Kaakro* or *kaklo* are dough balls made with ripe plantains and spices.

I N G R E D I E N T S

- **¹/₃ cup / 40 g soy flour**
- **³/₄ cup / 100 g flour**
- **1¹/₂ pounds / 750 g ripe plantains, mashed**
- **1 teaspoon fresh ginger, grated**
- **5 peppercorns, crushed**
- **1 onion, grated**
- **¹/₄ teaspoon paprika**
- **water**
- **oil**
- **salt and pepper**

1. In a bowl, mix together the soy and wheat flours.

2. Now place the mashed plantains in another bowl and put in the ginger, peppercorns, onion, paprika, salt and pepper.

3. Then add the flour mixture and a little water, some drops at a time, to make a smooth paste.

4. Heat enough oil for deep-frying – a depth of about 2 inches/ 5 cms in a pan or wok. Shape the flour and plantain mixture into small balls and cook them in the oil for a few minutes. Drain and serve hot with chutney or lemon wedges ∎

Akpith (Corn/maize and bean flour snack)

Serves 4-6

Corn/maize was introduced to Africa from Latin America by the Portuguese, mainly to provision their slave ships. The grain was quickly accepted because it grew rapidly and was undemanding in cultivation. The name 'maize' comes from *mahiz*, the word used by the Caribbean Taino Indians from whom the Europeans probably first learned about the crop. In North America the English settlers were shown it by local Indians. 'Corn' was a general name given to any grain, so they called it simply 'Indian corn'.

Columbus noted that maize was *'most tasty boiled, roasted or ground into flour'*. And in southern Ghana today a common food is *kenkey*, fermented corn/maize flour balls, wrapped in corn/maize leaves and steamed. *Akpith*, this recipe, is more straightforward.

I N G R E D I E N T S

1¹/₂ cups / 225 g corn/maize meal
¹/₂ cup / 60 g soy flour
1¹/₂ tablespoons baking powder
¹/₂ teaspoon chili powder +
sugar to taste
1 cup / 240 ml water
oil
salt and pepper

+ optional ingredient

1. In a large saucepan, boil the water and then mix in half of the corn/maize meal and all the soy flour to make a thick porridge. Add the baking powder, chili powder if using and sugar; season.

2. Cook this for 10 minutes over a low heat, stirring constantly. Then remove the pan and set aside to cool for 10 minutes or so.

3. At this point, mix in the remaining corn/maize meal and combine thoroughly, adding water to produce a stiff dough.

4. Now pour enough oil into a pan or wok to give a depth of around 2 inches/5 cms, and heat up. While it is warming mould the dough into balls about 1 inch/2.5 cms in diameter.

5. With the oil sizzling hot, slide 4 or 5 balls carefully into the pan and cook for 2-3 minutes until they are golden brown ■

MOZAMBIQUE

Cashew nuts piri-piri (Spicy cashew nuts)

Serves 4-6

According to some sources, *piri-piri* is the Portuguese word for the small red *malagueta* pepper. Others say *piri-piri* or *pili-pili* is a red peppercorn found in West Africa. Whatever its origins, in Mozambique *piri-piri* has become the name of the national dish and the wealth of hot, spicy dishes made with its fiery sauce. The sauce can also be used with peanuts, cooked beans or plantains (1-2 plantains, chopped into 1-inch/2.5-cm pieces).

I N G R E D I E N T S

1 clove garlic, crushed
¹/₂ teaspoon chili powder
squeeze of lemon
¹/₂ pound / 225 g cashew nuts
¹/₂ teaspoon salt
oil

1. Start by heating the oil in a heavy pan and then gently cook the garlic and chili powder for 2 minutes.

2. The lemon juice, salt and cashews can be added now. Then fry slowly, stirring all the time, until most of the sauce has dried as a coating on the nuts. Serve, or keep warm in the oven ■

Woman carrying bananas, Harare, Zimbabwe. *Photo: Jan Dago/Tony Stone Worldwide.*

SOUTH AFRICA

Sugar bean soup

Serves 4-6

In South Africa, the speckled sugar beans are a staple source of protein found in trading stores and supermarkets in black locations and rural districts. After soaking, they cook quickly which no doubt adds to their popularity – most rural black South Africans cook on open fires for which women collect firewood.

I N G R E D I E N T S

1 cup / 225 g sugar, pinto or borlotti beans, cooked

1 onion, sliced

1 quart / 1 liter stock

$^1/_2$-1 teaspoon thyme

1 tablespoon spinach or fresh parsley, chopped

oil

salt and pepper

1. Drain the beans and partially mash them, using a fork or potato masher.

2. Now heat the oil and sauté the onion in it. Then add the beans and the stock, the thyme and seasoning.

3. Bring the soup to the boil and simmer for 20-30 minutes before serving, garnished with the spinach or parsley ■

WEST AFRICA

Avocado and pineapple spread

Serves 4

Small, open-air restaurants in *Côte d'Ivoire* – one of the world's biggest pineapple producers – are called *maquis*. This means scrub or bush in French and was the name for the resistance movement in World War Two. In *Côte d'Ivoire*, a former French colony, local drinking places required authorization. To get around this, they moved to hidden courtyards and so earned their name. Today, however, they are legal eating houses.

I N G R E D I E N T S

1 avocado pear

a little lemon juice

a few pineapple pieces, fresh or canned

pinch of salt

1. Slice open the avocado pear and remove the stone. Then scoop the flesh into a bowl and add the lemon juice and salt. Mash well.

2. Spoon the mixture onto squares of wholemeal toast, crackers or corn chips and garnish with slivers of pineapple ■

WEST AFRICA

Kelewele (Fried plantains/savory bananas)

Serves 4

Kelewele or 'Killawilly', as some jokers have it, is simple and delicious. It uses many ingredients not originally found in Africa: bananas, ginger and pepper from south east Asia, and chili pepper from South America. But there was plenty of salt in the region – and this was the prized commodity in medieval times. In the 11th century the North African Berbers fought against the Ghanaian Empire (which lay to the north-west of modern Ghana) because they wanted access to its salt mines.

The banana pieces can be deep fried or cooked slowly on top of the cooker in a covered pan. They make an interesting snack or starter.

I N G R E D I E N T S

2 ripe plantains

2 teaspoons fresh ginger, grated

$^1/_2$ teaspoon chili powder

a little oil

salt and pepper

1. Peel the plantains and cut them into pieces about 1-inch/2.5-cms long.

2. Next put the ginger, chili, salt and pepper into a bowl and mix well. Then roll each chunk of plantain in the mixture.

3. Pour a little oil to coat the base of a heavy saucepan and when it is hot put in the plantain pieces. Stir them round so that they brown gently all over.

4. Now turn down the heat and cover the pan. Cook the plantains for about 30 minutes over a low heat stirring occasionally. Remove the lid for the last 10 minutes. Alternatively they can be cooked in a wok, using very hot oil to a depth of approximately 2 inches/5 cms, for 2-3 minutes ∎

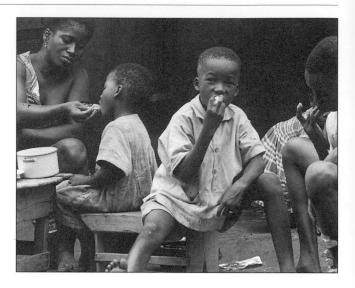

ZIMBABWE

Salted peanuts

Serves 2-4

'This is a delicious way to have salted peanuts without frying them in fat. You can also use other nuts or seeds instead of peanuts, and vary the flavoring by omitting the salt and mixing chili powder and/or *garam masala* into the water.'
Yvonne Burgess, Auchtermuchty, UK

I N G R E D I E N T S

1 cup / 125 g peanuts

$^1/_2$ teaspoon salt

$^1/_4$ cup / 60 ml warm water

1. Toast the peanuts in a frying pan, without oil, stirring frequently so that they do not burn.

2. When they are very hot, dissolve the salt in the warm water. Now pour this over the peanuts, and keep stirring all the while with the heat high. Suddenly all the water will disappear and the nuts will be coated with salt.

3. Continue to cook for 3 minutes to remove any moisture ∎

AFGHANISTAN

Yogurt and tomato soup

Serves 2-4

This recipe calls for *chaka* – yogurt which has been strained. You can make this by tying up ordinary yogurt in muslin and letting it drip for about 1 hour. Or you could buy ready-strained yogurt such as the Greek one found in many supermarkets.

In Afghanistan at mealtimes, people usually sit on cushions on the floor which is covered with beautiful rugs. Several people share one large dish, often rice served with two or three side dishes, including home-made chutneys and breads.

I N G R E D I E N T S

2 cloves garlic, crushed

2 tomatoes, chopped

1 cup / 225 g strained yogurt

1 tablespoon flour

1 cup / 240 ml milk

1 cup / 240 ml water

1/4 teaspoon turmeric

margarine

salt

1. Heat a little margarine in a saucepan and cook the garlic for a few minutes, taking care that it does not burn. Then add the tomatoes and stir as they cook.

2. In a bowl or blender, mix the strained yogurt with the flour and add the milk and water, turmeric and salt to taste.

3. When this is done, spoon the mixture into the saucepan containing the tomatoes and garlic and stir well.

4. Bring the soup slowly to the boil and simmer for 10 minutes or so, stirring until it thickens ■

BANGLADESH

Pianju (Onion snacks)

Serves 6

'Tea is rarely served in Bangladesh without some snacks, and one of the most popular is *pianju*, using onions and a flour paste made of lentils or garbanzos/chickpeas (called *gram* or *besan*). *Pianju* are also served in the hundreds of tiny tea-shops in the town. They are especially popular items for *iftar*, the meal taken to break the Muslim fast of Ramadan.

'It is best to cook them in a *korai* (wok). Note the use of bicarbonate of soda – this makes them really crispy.' *Meghna Guhathakurta, Dhaka, Bangladesh*

I N G R E D I E N T S

1 1/4 cups / 150 g gram flour or lentil flour

1/2 teaspoon bicarbonate of soda

1 onion, thinly sliced *

handful fresh cilantro/ coriander leaves, chopped

1 green chili, finely chopped

water

oil

salt

* You can use chopped fresh spinach as well or instead.

1. Shake the flour and bicarbonate of soda into a bowl and add enough water to make a gruel-like consistency.

2. Now put in the onion slices and/or spinach. Season with salt before adding the cilantro/coriander leaves and chili.

3. Next, heat enough oil in a wok (2 inches/5 cms or so) to deep-fry. Then take up some of the paste with a spoon and slide this mixture into the hot oil so it forms irregular ball shapes. Fry until they are golden and crisp.

4. Drain on kitchen paper, keep warm until all are ready, and then serve with tomato sauce or chutney (see p.122) ■

PEANUTS/GROUNDNUTS

"Peanuts, they're nice and hot. Peanuts, they taste a lot." That chorus comes from *The Peanut Vendor*, a song with a catchy Latin American beat set in Cuba – although it could be set anywhere, so worldwide a favorite are these 'nuts'.

In fact they are not nuts at all but rather a type of bean. The plant bears yellow flowers which turn into brown pods. These bury themselves beneath the soil to be dug up at harvest time. Rich in protein, oil and the vitamins B and E, peanuts make a major contribution to human nutrition – as snacks, peanut butter and groundnut stews.

There are two main types. One, found in Africa, is the Bambara groundnut which takes its name from the Bambara area in Mali. Today, these have largely been supplanted by the peanut (also called groundnut in Africa). The second is the more widely grown peanut which originated in the Mato Grosso region of Brazil.

The Spanish probably took some plants from Latin America to the Philippines and from there peanuts spread to Asia. Portuguese ships carried them to Africa around 1500, and on to India. It seems that peanuts came to North America in the 17th century from Africa, rather than from Latin America.

By the late 19th century peanuts had become very important in the US, India and West Africa. In West Africa, they played a major role in the 'legitimate commerce' that replaced the slave trade. They could be grown readily on a small scale by households with little capital, using family labor and traditional tools. Most of the crop was shipped to European countries for manufacture into cooking oil and soap, with the residue processed into animal cake.

With a shortage of oils in Europe after World War Two, colonial powers Britain and France sought to expand oil-seed production in their Third World gardens. Large tracts in the Dodoma region of what was then Tanganyika were planted with groundnuts, cultivated with heavy machinery – quite unsuitable for the fragile tropical soil. The scheme was a flop, leaving a legacy of disillusioned people, rusting machinery and exhausted soil in its wake.

By the 1950s, Senegal and Nigeria between them produced about 75 per cent of the world's groundnut exports. But the concentration on peanuts led to monoculture (where one crop is grown continuously) instead of the previous rotation system where millet and legumes such as peanuts replenished the soil with nutrients needed by the other. This led to deterioriation of the soil and it also meant there was less land to grow other food on.

But at least this cash crop can be eaten, unlike cotton. And groundnuts provide a good source of protein in Africa, as they do in other parts of the world. They are used in a variety of ways – Senegalese *mafé*, a groundnut stew for example; or peanut flour cakes, *kulikuli*, in Nigeria. In China peanut oil is prized for its flavor and high temperature tolerance.

The US is the world's largest consumer of peanuts – and 50 per cent of them are eaten as peanut butter. One claim is that this tasty sandwich-filler was invented in the 19th century by John Kellogg (brother of Will R 'Cornflakes' Kellogg). Others say it was George Washington Carver, acclaimed black scientist, who developed a range of products from the nut including peanut butter, flour and ink ■

CHINA

Spring rolls

Makes 15

'*Soy – what a wonderful food,*' said Kenny, a young Cantonese man, in a **New Internationalist** magazine article about soy beans, '*you name one other plant that you can make so many things from.*' Even US automobile magnate Henry Ford saw the plant's potential for his industry – as paint, body materials and oils. Soy beans in Asia are made into many food items, such as soy sauce used in this recipe. And because of their protein-rich value they were long ago classed as one of China's five 'sacred grains' along with rice, wheat, barley and millet.

I N G R E D I E N T S

¹/₂ pound / 225 g frozen spring roll pastry, thawed *

4 scallions/spring onions, thinly sliced

2-3 cloves garlic, crushed

1 teaspoon fresh ginger, grated

1 stick celery, finely chopped

1¹/₂ cups / 75 g mushrooms, finely chopped

1-2 tablespoons fresh cilantro/coriander leaves, chopped

1 cup / 50 g bean sprouts

¹/₂ tablespoon soy sauce

1 tablespoon sherry

¹/₄ teaspoon sugar

1 teaspoon cornstarch/cornflour

1 tablespoon cold water

oil

salt

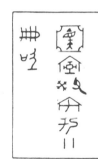

* Packet contains approximately 50 4-inch/10-cm square sheets. You could also use filo pastry sheets.

Heat oven to 250°F/130°C/Gas 1

1. To begin, heat 3 tablespoons of oil in a wok or wide frying pan. Put in the scallions/spring onions, garlic, ginger and cel-

cry and stir-fry until they are soft. Now add the mushrooms and cook in the same way for about 3 minutes.

2. The cilantro/coriander leaves, bean sprouts, soy sauce, sherry and sugar can be put in now. Cook, stirring briskly, until everything has combined.

3. If the mixture looks too wet, make a thin paste with the cornstarch/cornflour and water and stir this into the vegetables. Let it cook for a minute or two and then season. Now take the pan from the heat and set aside.

4. Place a little of the mixture in the middle of the spring roll sheet. Fold the sides inwards and then roll it into a cylinder shape. Seal edges with a little water.

5. With the rolls made, pour 2 inches/5 cms of oil – enough for deep-frying – into the wok or pan.

6. When the oil is very hot, but not smoking, fry the rolls (about 4-6 at a time) until golden on all sides. Drain on kitchen paper and then keep them warm in the oven while you cook the remainder. Serve with soy sauce ∎

Azuki bean soup

Serves 2-4

Shiny red Azuki, Aduki or Adzuki beans probably originated in China. They have a nutty flavor and sweetness which can be enhanced by the addition of a little sugar or coconut milk. So warn your table-mates or try serving it as a dessert – in China it is often served at the end of a meal. In Malaysia the thin sweet soup is eaten as a snack, usually purchased from the street hawkers' stalls.

I N G R E D I E N T S

$^1/_2$ cup / 110 g azuki beans

2 tablespoons rice

1 tablespoon sugar

$1^1/_2$ quarts / 1.5 liters water

pinch of salt

1. Place the beans and the rice in a heavy saucepan, pour in the water and bring to the boil. When it reaches boiling point, turn down the heat, remove the lid and simmer for 2 minutes or so. Then turn off the heat and leave the pot to stand, uncovered, for 1 hour.

2. After that, cover the pan and bring to the boil again and then let the rice and beans simmer slowly for 1 hour. Keep the lid on, but leave it slightly ajar.

3. When ready, blend the soup, pouring in more liquid if necessary to obtain the consistency you prefer. Add sugar and salt and blend again. The soup can be served hot or chilled, with the addition of cream or yogurt if liked ■

HONG KONG

Noodle soup

Serves 4

Downtown Kowloon, on the mainland just across from Hong Kong island, is best viewed from one of the many Black Star ferries. They buzz around the harbour, plying back and forth through remarkably clean water – there's an on-the-spot fine for throwing litter in the sea. And where the ferry docks in Kowloon there are rows of street hawkers dispensing quick meals for commuters. Along with the food, such as this soup, you will receive bags of cheerfulness and street-wise chat.

In this recipe, use the thin, clear noodles made from mung bean or soy bean starch. They are called 'bean threads', 'Chinese vermicelli', 'shining noodles' – available from Asian stores.

I N G R E D I E N T S

2 carrots, chopped into matchstick size

1 cup / 110 g cabbage, shredded

$^3/_4$ cup / 75 g bamboo shoots, finely sliced

2 tomatoes, sliced

$^1/_2$ cup / 75 g bean thread noodles

1 quart / 1 liter stock or water

$1^1/_2$ cups / 75 g bean sprouts

2 scallions/spring onions, finely chopped

3 tablespoons soy sauce

oil

salt and pepper

1. Heat some oil in a saucepan or wok and briskly fry the carrots, cabbage, bamboo shoots and tomatoes with a little salt for 5 minutes, stirring all the time.

2. Now pour in the stock, stir well, and then add the noodles. Bring the soup to the boil and then let it simmer for 30 minutes.

3. The bean sprouts and chopped scallions/spring onions can go in now. Then spoon in the soy sauce, season the soup and let the flavors mingle as it cooks gently for a further 10 minutes before serving ■

1. Heat the margarine in a pan and when it is ready put in the potato. Stir-fry it for a minute or so and then add the banana, cooking them together for another minute.

2. Meanwhile, halve the grapes and remove the seeds (or use seedless grapes). Now put in the apple cubes followed by the orange segments, grapes, chaat masala and pepper. Stir well to mix all the ingredients.

3. Cook for a couple of minutes and then pour in the lemon juice, mix, and serve at once ■

INDIA

Phalon ka chaat (Fruit snack)

Serves 2-4

'*Chaat* is a tangy, spicy snack from the Punjab where there are many fruit and vegetable *chaats*. Steaming hot *chaats* are usually served at food stalls in cups made from dried leaves, with a couple of toothpicks to impale the segments of fruit or vegetables. The dish can also accompany main meals.' *Dinyar Godrej, Oxford, UK*

I N G R E D I E N T S

1 potato, cubed and parboiled

1 banana, sliced

$^1/_2$ cup / 100 g grapes

1 apple, cubed

1 orange, in segments

1 teaspoon chaat masala *

1 tablespoon lemon juice

1 tablespoon margarine

pepper

* This spicy flavoring powder can be found at most Asian grocery stores.

Boats laden with vegetables, Dhaka, Bangladesh. *Photo: Sharfuddin Ahmed/Drik Picture Library.*

INDIA

Spinach bhajias (Fritters)

Serves 6

Popular appetizers, these deep-fried delights gain their distinctive flavor from the use of gram (garbanzo/chickpea) flour, also known as *besan*. Hindi speakers call them *bhajias* whereas the stouter Punjabi versions are called *pakoras*. If the filling is rolled into a ball and coated in batter it becomes a *bonda* or *bada*. In south India the closest equivalent is the *vada* made of ground lentils and eaten with coconut chutney.

Try making the *bhajias* with slices of potato and onion rings, and serve with tomato or tamarind chutney. Delicious as they are, however, with their high fat content you may not want to eat them too frequently.

I N G R E D I E N T S

1¼ cups / 150 g gram flour

½ teaspoon ground coriander

¼ teaspoon chili powder

pinch of bicarbonate of soda

12 spinach leaves, sliced

½ cup / 110 g yogurt

lemon juice +

½ teaspoon garam masala +

water

oil

salt

+ optional ingredients

1. Place all the ingredients, except the spinach, water and yogurt, into a bowl.

2. Mix them with enough water to make a pouring batter and then add the spinach and combine it well. Heat the oil for deep frying in a wok, to a depth of roughly 2 inches/5 cms.

3. When the oil is sizzling hot, spoon in some of the bhajia mixture and let it take its own irregular shape. Fry until it is golden brown.

4. Repeat until all the batter is finished, keeping the cooked ones hot.

5. When ready to serve, mix the yogurt in a small bowl with a judicious sprinkling of salt and enough water to give a sauce-like consistency (this will depend on the kind of yogurt you are using – some are runny enough without the addition of water).

6. Now arrange the hot bhajias on a plate and pour the yogurt sauce over. Top with tamarind chutney (see p.122) ∎

IN ALL RECIPES
● PEPPER AND SALT ARE TO TASTE.
● CHILI AND SUGAR ARE GIVEN AS GUIDE QUANTITIES ONLY.
VARY TO TASTE.
● MEASURES FOR BEANS AND GRAINS REFER TO DRY INGREDIENTS.

INDONESIA

Stir-fried tempeh

Serves 4

'*Tempeh* is everywhere in Indonesia, and I'm addicted to its nutty flavor. After a long hot working day I would return home to a *tempeh*, lettuce and tomato sandwich, an adaption of the American BLT (bacon, lettuce and tomato) which Indonesian friends have grown to like too.' *Nancy Bergan, Jakarta, Indonesia*

Tempeh is an ancient Indonesian food, usually made from fermented soy beans but also from other beans or grains. Weight for weight it contains almost as much usable protein as chicken. *Tempeh* is sold as cakes with the tastes and textures varying according to the ingredients and how long they are fermented for. Like bean-curd/tofu, it lends itself to other flavors. In this recipe the *tempeh* pieces are dipped into the sauce before frying or baking.

I N G R E D I E N T S

5-6 cloves garlic, crushed

1 teaspoon ground coriander

2-3 tablespoons soy sauce

$^1/_2$ pound / 225 g tempeh

oil

water

salt and pepper

Heat oven to 375°F/190°C/Gas 5 (if using; see (3) below)

1. First mix the garlic, ground coriander, soy sauce and salt with enough water to make a thin paste.

2. Now cut the tempeh into sticks or small cubes and place some in the sauce to marinate for a few minutes.

3. To cook, either lay the tempeh on a baking sheet and cook in the oven for 15-20 minutes or fry as follows.

4. Heat up the oil in a wok or frying pan and then transfer the soaked tempeh pieces, retaining as much of the marinade as you can.

5. Put in some more tempeh to soak while you stir-fry the first batch for 5-6 minutes until they are crisp. Drain on kitchen paper and then serve, or keep hot while you cook the rest in the same way ■

MALAYSIA

Samosas

Makes about 15

Spicy and fresh, these Indian appetizers appear around the world in slightly different guises. In Malaysia, they were probably introduced by Tamils from south India who had been brought across to work Malaysia's rubber plantations. The

Chinese are the largest minority in Malaysia with around 36 per cent of the population. The culinary fusion of Indian samosas with Chinese spring roll pastry results in a tiny but tasty manifestation of the mixed cultures in the kitchen.

I N G R E D I E N T S

¹/₄ pound / 110 g frozen spring roll pastry, thawed *

1 potato, diced

¹/₂ cup / 35 g mixture of cauliflower, carrots, cabbage, finely chopped

1 tablespoon peas

1 tablespoon cilantro/coriander leaves, chopped

¹/₂ teaspoon fresh ginger, grated

¹/₂ onion, finely sliced

2 cloves garlic, crushed

¹/₂ teaspoon green chili

¹/₄ teaspoon turmeric

1 teaspoon garam masala

1-2 teaspoons lime or lemon juice

oil

salt

1 lime or lemon

* For samosas, the sheets should measure 6 x 4 inches/
15 x 10 cms.

1. Start by boiling some water in a saucepan and then drop in the chopped potato and other vegetables, including the peas.

2. Let them boil for a few minutes until they are almost cooked and then drain and transfer them to a bowl.

3. The vegetables can now be mixed with the cilantro/coriander leaves, ginger, onion, garlic, chili, turmeric, garam masala, lemon or lime juice and seasoning.

4. Cut the pastry (if necessary) to produce strips measuring 6 x 4 inches/15 x 10 cms. Pile some of the mixture onto the middle of the strip; fold over one end, then the other to make a triangular pocket. Stick down the ends with a little water or beaten egg.

5. Heat about 2 inches/5 cms of oil in a wok or deep-fry pan and cook for a few minutes until the samosas are golden brown. Serve hot with wedges of lemon or lime ∎

THAILAND

Spicy tomato and bean-curd/tofu soup

Serves 4

'Protein without legs' is how soy is described in China and indeed, acre for acre, soy beans (from which bean-curd/tofu is made) yield about 15 times more protein than beef. In this recipe, use 'silken' tofu if you can for its delicate smoothness – otherwise ordinary bean-curd/tofu will do.

I N G R E D I E N T S

4 tomatoes, chopped

2¹/₂ cups / 375 g bean-curd/tofu, chopped

2 tablespoons soy sauce

1³/₄ cups / 420 ml coconut milk

1 tablespoon lemon juice

¹/₂ -1 teaspoon curry powder

2 tablespoons cilantro/coriander leaves, chopped

1. Place the tomatoes and bean-curd/tofu in a blender and whisk them together, or mix well in a bowl.

2. Add the soy sauce, coconut milk, lemon juice and curry powder and either blend or combine all the ingredients.

3. Now transfer the soup to a saucepan; add 1 tablespoon of the chopped cilantro/coriander leaves and slowly bring to the boil, uncovered.

4. At this point, turn down the heat and let the soup bubble gently for 10 minutes before serving with the remaining cilantro/coriander leaves scattered on top ∎

1. Put the pumpkin pieces in a pan with a little water and bring to the boil. Cook gently until they are soft.

2. In another pan melt the margarine and fry the onion for a few minutes until it begins to turn golden and then add the garlic. Fry that for a few moments, put in the tomato and cook for a little longer.

3. Now shake in the flour; stir well to distribute it evenly. The cooked pumpkin goes in now and then gradually pour on the milk, stirring as you do so to mix the ingredients.

4. Sprinkle on the sugar if using and the chili powder; season and then simmer the soup for 15-20 minutes, stirring now and again as it thickens ∎

BRAZIL

Quibebe (Pumpkin soup)

Serves 4

The main staple foods in Brazil are *arroz* (rice), *feijão* (black beans) and *farinha* (cassava/manioc flour) which is often sprinkled on top of food, rather like parmesan cheese. A distinctive cooking oil is used in the north-east, Bahian region. This is *dendê*, made from the fragrant oil of the *dendê* palm tree. And one of Brazil's most popular soft drinks is *guaraná*, made from the berry of an Amazonian plant bearing the same name.

I N G R E D I E N T S

1 pound / 450 g pumpkin, peeled and cut into 1/2-inch/ 1.5-cm chunks

1 onion, sliced

1-2 cloves garlic, crushed

1 tomato, sliced

2 tablespoons flour

1 3/4 cups / 420 ml milk

1/4 teaspoon sugar +

1/4 teaspoon chili powder

1 tablespoon margarine

salt and pepper

+ optional ingredient

CARIBBEAN

Avocado soup

Serves 4-6

While in the West we may think of avocado pears as luxury food, they are known as 'butter of the poor' in some tropical parts where they grow in abundance all year round providing a handy source of protein and vitamins. Avocadoes were first cultivated in Central America 7,000 years ago and today the major producer is the United States, with South Africa and Israel having large export trades.

This soup is very easy and quick to make.

I N G R E D I E N T S

3 avocado pears

stalks of 2 scallions/spring onions, finely chopped

1 tablespoon lime or lemon juice

2 1/2 cups / 590 ml milk *

salt and pepper

* This makes a very thick, creamy soup, so have more milk at hand if you think you may want a thinner mixture.

1. Begin by slicing the avocadoes in half lengthwise and scooping the pulp into a bowl. Mash to a purée with a fork.

2. Now put in most of the chopped scallions/spring onions

– was assured. Now that's all changing as the General Agreement on Tariffs and Trade (GATT), dominated by the US and Western industrialized countries, seeks to operate a free market for these foods.

INGREDIENTS

1 egg-plant/aubergine, sliced

1 teaspoon onion, grated

1 clove garlic, crushed

1 tomato, finely chopped

$1/2$ teaspoon sugar

2 tablespoons vinegar

2 tablespoons oil

water

salt and pepper

1. Start by cooking the egg-plant/aubergine slices in boiling salted water for a few minutes until tender. Drain and put into a bowl and then mash them.

2. Now add the onion, garlic, tomato, sugar, vinegar, oil, salt and pepper and beat to make a creamy dip consistency.

3. Chill and then serve with lemon wedges ∎

(hold some back for the garnish) and the lime or lemon juice and mix well.

3. The milk can be poured in now, a little at a time. Combine it with the other ingredients as you do so to make a smooth liquid, or put the mixture in a blender. Season and top with a little chopped scallion/spring onion ∎

Egg-plant/aubergine spread

Serves 4-6

Calypsos, cricket, rastafarians, rum, beaches – some of the images held in the West about the arc of islands in the Caribbean. But many of the islands are suffering their worst times economically. Under their colonizers (including Britain, France and Spain) they were transformed into plantations for sugar and bananas. Their market – in the colonizing country

> **IN ALL RECIPES**
> ● PEPPER AND SALT ARE TO TASTE.
> ● CHILI AND SUGAR ARE GIVEN AS GUIDE QUANTITIES ONLY.
> VARY TO TASTE.
> ● MEASURES FOR BEANS AND GRAINS REFER TO DRY INGREDIENTS.

DOMINICAN REPUBLIC

Cream of watercress soup

Serves 4

The Dominican Republic shares its island with Haiti – the island once known as Hispaniola where Columbus made landfall in 1492. The capital, Santa Domingo, has the oldest cathedral in the Americas: a lasting symbol of the power of the Church and of the blood shed in the name of Christianity.

Nutmegs, used in the recipe, came originally from the Molucca Islands (Indonesia) and were not transplanted to other parts of the tropics until the last part of the 18th century. Today, the Dominican Republic's neighbor Grenada and Indonesia are the world's main producers.

INGREDIENTS

3 tablespoons flour
2¹/₂ cups / 590 ml stock
1 onion, finely chopped
¹/₂ pound / 225 g watercress, chopped
1³/₄ cups / 420 ml coconut milk
¹/₂ teaspoon nutmeg, grated
¹/₂ teaspoon chili, seeded and finely chopped
1 cup / 220 g cream or yogurt +
1 tablespoon chives, chopped
2 tablespoons margarine
salt and pepper

+ optional ingredient

1. First of all sift the flour into a small basin and add enough of the stock to make a smooth paste.

2. Then heat the margarine and cook the onion until it is soft and golden. Now add the watercress and let this sweat until it becomes limp.

3. Pour in the coconut milk and stir the ingredients together. Bring to the boil, uncovered, and then spoon in the flour paste before continuing to simmer for a further 3 minutes or so.

4. After this, add the stock and also the nutmeg and chili. Allow the soup to simmer for a few minutes more and then season to taste.

5. Remove from the heat and when it has cooled slightly put the soup through a sieve or liquidize it – or you can leave it, with its varied texture, and serve.

6. If you have blended the soup, pour it back into a pan and heat up. Place the cream or yogurt and the chopped chives in small bowls on the table. Serve the soup, inviting people to help themselves to the cream or yogurt and chives ■

> **IN ALL RECIPES**
> ● PEPPER AND SALT ARE TO TASTE.
> ● CHILI AND SUGAR ARE GIVEN AS GUIDE QUANTITIES ONLY.
> VARY TO TASTE.
> ● MEASURES FOR BEANS AND GRAINS REFER TO DRY INGREDIENTS.

EL SALVADOR

Sopa de frijoles (Bean soup)

Serves 4-6

El Salvador's name – The Savior – has a hollow ring after the years of ferocious civil war in the country, sparked by unfair land distribution and abuses of human rights. Although the killing of Archbishop Oscar Romero at the cathedral in San Salvador in 1981 was an event which caught the world's attention, thousands of ordinary people have died in a war in which the United States supported the military government's

thuggery. In the 1990s, at last, there is peace and attempts at rebuilding shattered lives and the economy.

The main food crops are corn/maize, beans and rice: staples throughout the region.

INGREDIENTS

1 cup / 225 g red kidney or haricot beans, cooked (do not drain)

1 onion, chopped

$1/4$ teaspoon cloves, crushed or powdered

$1/4$ teaspoon cinnamon

$1/2$ teaspoon thyme

$1/2$ teaspoon oregano

6 slices bread, cut into quarters

lemon wedges

oil

salt and pepper

1. When the beans are cooked, take out about half of them and mash in a bowl. Then return them to the pan.

2. In a different cooking pan, heat the oil and sauté the onion for a few minutes until it is golden. When it is ready, put it in with the beans.

3. Now add the spices and seasoning as well and gently boil the bean mixture in about 3 cups/700 ml of the cooking water for 10 minutes.

4. While that is going on, heat up some more oil and fry the bread pieces until they are brown; then turn them over and cook on the other side.

5. Place the bread in the bottom of individual soup bowls and ladle the bean soup over. Serve right away, with the lemon wedges ■

Man using traditional digging stick in potato field, Peru. *Photo: Hansruedi Dörig.*

GUATEMALA

Corn/maize soup

Serves 4

Mayan Indians make up about 60 per cent of Guatemala's population, as they live in the mountainous region of the country and were never completely dominated by the Spanish *conquistadores*. But in recent years military rulers have been more successful in crushing peasant opposition.

Coffee, bananas and cotton are the country's leading exports, followed by the spice, cardamom, and sugar. Guatemala's highlands are the source of a variety of corn/maize, known as 'flint'.

I N G R E D I E N T S

kernels from 3 fresh corn cobs, or 1 can sweetcorn kernels

1 onion, sliced finely

2 tablespoons flour

2¹/₂ cups / 590 ml milk

1 tablespoon margarine

salt and pepper

1. If using fresh corn, cook it in boiling water for 5-10 minutes until tender. Drain, but keep the water. With canned corn, keep the liquid also when you drain the kernels.

2. Next, melt the margarine in a pan and cook the onion until soft. Now sprinkle in the flour, mixing well. Cook for a couple of minutes, stirring all the time.

3. When you have done that, remove the pan from the heat and slowly pour in the milk, stirring as you do so to give a smooth consistency.

4. The corn kernels go in now, along with the salt and pepper and about ¹/₂ cup/120 ml of the drained water. Bring the soup to the boil gently, stirring as the mixture thickens, and then simmer for a few minutes. Check the seasoning and serve ■

JAMAICA

Pigeon pea/gunga soup

Serves 4

Pigeon peas, named perhaps for their gray-brown speckled colors which resemble pigeon plumage, are probably native to Africa although they had reached tropical Asia in pre-historic times. They were conveyed to the Americas probably by the Portuguese. Known by the name *gunga* in the Caribbean, they were a staple food for the slaves and they are still common fare in the region and southern states of the US.

This dish is creamy, with a hint of sweetness from the coconut milk.

I N G R E D I E N T S

1 onion, chopped

1 cup / 225 g pigeon peas, cooked

1 cup / 150 g canned sweetcorn kernels

2¹/₂ cups / 590 ml coconut milk

1 tablespoon margarine

salt and pepper

1. Begin by melting the margarine and cooking the onion until it is transparent.

2. Then put in the pigeon peas and corn kernels and cook them slowly for 10 minutes. Now mash them, or transfer to a blender, and then pour in the coconut milk and season to taste. When the ingredients are well mixed, return them to the cooking pan.

3. Heat the soup very gently for 20 minutes and then serve it hot with bread ■

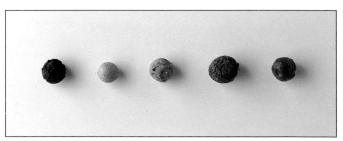

MEXICO

Red bell pepper soup

Serves 2-4

Chili powder, red and cayenne peppers, Tabasco, paprika, sweet or bell peppers and pimientos are all derived from the pod-like berry of various species of *capsicum*. They were the Americas' famous contribution to the world's spice cupboard, and according to some sources, are called 'pepper' because Columbus thought (hoped) he had reached India and found the foremost spice of that time – *piper*, from which we get peppercorns. But *piper* comes from south-west India.

INGREDIENTS

1 onion, sliced

2 red bell peppers, chopped

2^1/$_2$ cups / 590 ml vegetable stock

1 cup / 240 ml tomato juice

1 chili

oil

salt and pepper

1. Heat the oil to begin with and then gently cook the onion until it is soft and golden.

2. Now put it together with the chopped bell peppers and some of the stock into a blender to make a purée.

3. Return this to the pan and pour in the tomato juice and enough of the remaining stock to give the consistency you prefer. Season and then drop in the whole chili. Cover the saucepan and let the soup simmer for 10 minutes before removing the chili and then serve hot ■

Guacamole and nachos chips

Serves 6

'In October 1990 Andrés came from Mexico to study in England, missing our long hot summer. He soon began to miss his homeland. It emerged that, other than the weather, part of the problem was the "unimaginative English food". Since I love cooking and sharing food with others I felt we could tackle this.

'Initially Andrés had a little trouble with the concept of a vegetarian who eats no fish or chicken: it appears that the few vegetarians there are in Mexico usually eat both. Once we had resolved this however, we realized that some Mexican food is vegetarian anyway and wonderful meals can be created.' (See also recipes on pps. 93, 129 and 130.) *Caitlin Buck and José Andrés Christen, Leeds, UK and Mexico*

INGREDIENTS

4 avocado pears

1 onion, finely sliced or grated

1 tablespoon fresh cilantro/coriander or parsley, chopped

1-2 green chili peppers, finely chopped

juice of 1 lime or lemon

salt

pack of nachos chips

1. Cut the avocadoes in half, discard the stones and scoop the flesh into a bowl with a spoon.

2. Mash it well with a fork until there are no lumps. Now put in the onion, cilantro/coriander or parsley leaves and chili and mix well to blend all the ingredients.

3. Pour in the lime or lemon juice and add salt to taste. Serve at once, with the nachos chips in a dish alongside ■

EGYPT

Dip with broad beans and lentils

Serves 4-6

This is a different way to serve beans and lentils. It also makes a useful addition to a range of starters for a meal. Some of today's staple foods, including beans and lentils, have been grown in the Middle East since earliest times. And Esau, in the Bible, sold his birthright to his brother Jacob *'for a pottage of lentils'*.

INGREDIENTS

1 cup / 175 g butter beans or dried broad beans, cooked

2 tablespoons red lentils, cooked

2 cloves garlic, crushed

4 tablespoons lemon juice

¹/₄ teaspoon ground cumin

1 tablespoon fresh parsley, chopped

pinch of paprika

3 tablespoons olive oil

salt

1. Mash the beans and lentils together in a bowl with a fork or use a blender. Then add garlic, lemon juice, cumin, salt and 2 tablespoons of the oil to make a coherent paste.

2. Scoop the mixture into a shallow dish and pour the rest of the oil over it; garnish with the parsley and paprika and serve with hot pitta bread and sticks of carrot and celery ■

Michoteta (Cucumber salad with cheese)

Serves 4-6

This salad would normally use *feta* (sheep's or goat's milk cheese) but you could use ricotta, cottage or curd cheese instead. As *feta* cheese is quite salty (it is cured and stored in brine) you will probably not need to add any salt.

INGREDIENTS

¹/₂ pound / 225 g feta

2 tablespoons lemon juice

2 tablespoons olive oil

2 inches / 5 cms cucumber, finely cubed

¹/₂ onion, finely sliced

¹/₂ teaspoon ground cumin

pinch of paprika

pepper

1. First place the cheese in a bowl and break it up with a fork. Now add drops of the lemon juice and oil, a little at a time, and turn them in with the cheese.

2. The cucumber, onion and cumin go in now, together with the seasoning.

3. Sprinkle on the paprika before serving. This salad is good either as a starter with pitta bread or as an accompaniment to a main dish ■

gently. When that is done, sprinkle the dill or fennel and parsley into the bowl and mix them in.

3. Chill, and before serving drizzle with a little oil. Hand round hot pitta bread to accompany the dip ■

MIDDLE EAST

Hummus bi tahini (Garbanzo/chickpea dip)

Serves 4-6

'In 1991 I went to Israel and participated in a Peace Walk from Jerusalem to Amman, Jordan – about 120 kilometers. There were people from 13 countries ranging from 16 years old to 63 (me). On the road our most frequently eaten food was hummus and pitta bread with fresh cucumbers and tomatoes...' *Jean McLaren, Gabriola Island, BC, Canada*

I N G R E D I E N T S

1¹/₄ cups / 225 g garbanzos/ chickpeas, cooked (keep the water)

3 cloves garlic, crushed

a little milk or retained cooking water

1 tablespoon tahina *

juice of 2 lemons

¹/₂ tablespoon fresh parsley, chopped

¹/₄ teaspoon paprika

olive oil

salt and pepper

* Paste made from ground sesame seeds, available from wholefood stores.

1. Put the cooked garbanzos/chickpeas into a blender with the garlic, and some of the retained cooking water or milk. You may need to do this in two or three lots as the garbanzos/ chickpeas are quite stiff. Add the milk or retained cooking water as necessary to make a smooth, creamy consistency.

2. Now spoon in the tahina, add the lemon juice and the salt and pepper. Whizz the mixture once more and check the fla-

Gibneh beydah (Goat's cheese dip)

Serves 4

Egypt's economy relies on oil exports, migrant worker remittances, tourism and tolls collected from the Suez Canal. The Gulf War forced many migrant workers home and tourism was also badly hit. Oranges, cotton and potatoes are the main agricultural exports, but the country has to import about 65 per cent of its food.

I N G R E D I E N T S

¹/₄ pound / 110 g feta or other goat's cheese

2 tablespoons yogurt

a little milk

¹/₂ tablespoon lemon juice

1 tablespoon fresh dill or fennel, finely chopped

1 tablespoon fresh parsley, finely chopped

olive oil

1. In a bowl, mix the feta or goat's cheese with the yogurt until the mixture is smooth and creamy.

2. Now pour on a little milk, oil and lemon juice, stirring

vors, adding more salt, tahina or lemon juice as desired.

3. Turn the hummus into a shallow bowl and pour on a little olive oil to cover the surface with a thin film, scatter the parsley over and sprinkle on the paprika. Serve with hot pitta bread and chopped cucumber, carrots, fennel root, bell pepper or celery sticks ■

Baba ganoush (Egg-plant/aubergine and tahina dip)

Serves 4

Garden egg, *brinjal* and *batinjan* are some of the other names for the egg-plant or aubergine. This popular vegetable, a 'poor person's caviar', is indigenous to India and was taken by the Arabs to Spain and by the Spaniards to South America.

Baba ganoush makes an interesting start to a meal, with the pungent tastes of tahina and egg-plant/aubergine bound together as a creamy dip.

I N G R E D I E N T S

1 egg-plant/aubergine

1-2 cloves garlic, crushed

1 tablespoon tahina

pinch of ground cumin

juice of ¹/₂ lemon

1 tablespoon fresh parsley, chopped

a few black olives

salt

Heat oven to 350°F/180°C/Gas 4 (if using; see (1) below)

1. First, cook the aubergine in the oven or under the grill for 10 minutes or so until it is soft but not burnt. Then scoop out the pulp into a bowl and mash it with a fork, or put it into a blender.

2. Now add the garlic, tahina, cumin, salt and a few drops of lemon juice. Blend again or combine well and add more of the juice, salt or other ingredients until you have the consistency and taste you like.

3. Place the baba ganoush in a shallow bowl and scatter the fresh parsley on top. Then add the black olives before serving as a dip with pitta bread or chopped raw vegetables ■

IN ALL RECIPES
● **PEPPER AND SALT ARE TO TASTE.**
● **CHILI AND SUGAR ARE GIVEN AS GUIDE QUANTITIES ONLY.**
VARY TO TASTE.
● **MEASURES FOR BEANS AND GRAINS REFER TO DRY INGREDIENTS.**

SYRIA

Shourabat adas (Lentil soup)

Serves 4-6

Syria may well have been the region where the biblical Garden of Eden was sited. Certainly it had, and has, an abundance of foods: wheat, barley, millet, corn/maize, lentils; fruit such as figs, pomegranates and apricots, and vegetables including tomatoes and potatoes.

I N G R E D I E N T S

1 cup / 225 g red, green or brown lentils

3 cups / 700 ml stock or water

2 onions, finely chopped

1 carrot, sliced

2 cloves garlic, crushed

1 teaspoon ground cumin

juice of 1 lemon

olive oil

salt and pepper

lemon wedges

1. Place the lentils in a pan with the stock or water, add one of the onions and the carrot and bring to the boil. Then turn down the heat and let the soup simmer for 20-30 minutes until the lentils are very soft.

2. Now transfer the mixture to a blender or push it through a sieve or you can simply beat it well in the saucepan with a wooden spoon.

3. After that, return the soup to the heat and add the cumin, lemon juice and seasoning.

4. Let it simmer softly for 10 minutes and while that is doing, heat the oil and fry the remaining onion until it is translucent. Add the garlic and cook this until both ingredients are just turning golden brown.

5. Serve the soup in bowls garnished with the onion and garlic, with the lemon wedges for extra zest ∎

Abou ganouje (Spicy egg-plant/aubergine salad)

Serves 4-6

Cultivation of olive trees, whose fruits yield the oil, probably started 6,000 years ago in the eastern Mediterranean area. The straggly wild plant was widely distributed but it took the enterprise and mercantile genius of the Syrians and Palestinians to transform it into the thornless, compact tree with fruits rich in oil we know today.

This salad is best made at least an hour before you want to serve it so that the dressing can be absorbed.

I N G R E D I E N T S

2-3 egg-plants/aubergines

1 green bell pepper, finely sliced

2-3 tomatoes, finely sliced

1 onion, finely sliced

4 tablespoons olive oil

juice of 1-2 lemons

2 cloves garlic, crushed

$1/2$ teaspoon chili powder

1 teaspoon ground cumin

1 tablespoon fresh parsley, chopped

salt and pepper

Heat oven to 350°F/180°C/Gas 4

1. Start by cooking the egg-plants/aubergines in the oven; they are ready when they feel soft (about 10-15 minutes). Set aside to cool.

2. Now cut them in half and scoop out the pulp. Chop or slice into small pieces and then, in a bowl, add it to the bell pepper, tomatoes and onion.

3. Join the olive oil to the lemon juice and add the garlic, chili, cumin, half of the parsley, and seasoning. Pour the dressing over the salad and mix it round well before garnishing with the rest of the parsley ∎

MAIN COURSES

Food being put on roof to dry, Nepal. *Photo: Osmond/Tony Stone Worldwide.*

coconut milk, stirring to blend the ingredients.

4. Cover the pan and leave it to simmer for 10 minutes before garnishing with the remaining cilantro/coriander leaves or parsley. Serve with rice, nshima (p.112) or phulkas (p.121) ■

EAST AFRICA

Maharagwe (Spiced beans in coconut milk)

Serves 4-6

The ninth-century rise of Islam led on to the development of coastal towns in East Africa to which traders came from Persia, Arabia and India seeking leopard-skins, tortoise-shell, timber and above all ivory. Sultanates were established in Mogadishu, Kilwa and Zanzibar and by the 15th century these were rich towns, with trading also in gold. The sultans' power waned with the arrival of the Portuguese in the 16th century, but Arab influence survives in the Swahili coastal culture: food is one example.

INGREDIENTS

1 onion, chopped

1 cup / 225 g cowpeas/black-eyed, pinto or rosecoco beans, cooked

3 tomatoes, chopped

1¹/₂ teaspoons turmeric

1 teaspoon chili powder

1 tablespoon fresh cilantro/coriander leaves or parsley, chopped

1¹/₂ cups / 360 ml coconut milk

oil

salt

1. Using a deep, heavy pan, heat the oil and cook the onion gently until soft and golden.

2. Partially mash the beans with a fork and then spoon them into the onion. Add the chopped tomatoes and mix well.

3. Now put in the turmeric and chili powder, seasoning and half the cilantro/coriander leaves. After that, pour in the

ETHIOPIA

Yemesirkik (Lentil wat/stew)

Serves 4-6

Laurens van der Post, traveller and author, wrote that the Ethiopian system of fasting – refraining from meat and fish – especially during the eight weeks of Lent before Easter has *'compelled (them) to concentrate on vegetarian substitutes for meat as no other culture in Africa has done'.* This has produced a rich variety of vegetable *wats* or stews using a spice paste (*berberé*) combined with lentils, as in this recipe, or with other vegetables and pulses.

INGREDIENTS

1 onion, chopped

2-3 teaspoons berberé paste *

2 cloves garlic, crushed

2 cups / 450 g brown or red lentils, cooked

water

oil

salt

* See p.106.

1. Heat 1 tablespoon of oil in a heavy pan and sauté the onion. When it is soft and turning golden, add the berberé paste and garlic and mix in well.

2. Cook for a minute or two and then add a little water and 2 more tablespoons of oil.

3. Mash the cooked lentils and put these into the onion mix; stir often so that the mixture does not burn.

4. Now pour in a little more water and sprinkle in salt to taste. Cook for 5-10 minutes longer to let the flavors expand and then set aside to cool. Serve warm or cool with funkaso (*millet pancakes,* p.108) ∎

Shiro wat (Peanut/groundnut stew)

Serves 4

War and droughts color the West's image of Ethiopia, although the country now appears to be on the road to democracy. But of course Ethiopia has many other facets. It is a major center of 'genetic diversity': the precursors of many of today's food plants grow there. One such is *arabica* coffee, probably first cultivated in the sixth century. This is Ethiopia's main export earner although it has been badly hit by the country's internal problems as well as by falling world prices in the early 1990s.

INGREDIENTS

2 cups / 225 g raw peanuts

1 onion, finely sliced

2 teaspoons berberé paste *

2 tablespoons tomato purée

1 egg, beaten

2¹/₂ cups / 590 ml water

oil or margarine

salt

* See p.106.

1. Put the nuts into a blender and grind them to a regular smooth texture.

2. Now heat the margarine or oil in a saucepan and gently sauté the onion before adding the berberé paste and tomato purée. Mix these ingredients well and cook for a minute or two, stirring all the time.

3. Spoon in the beaten egg next and then gradually add the ground peanuts. When this is done, begin to pour in the water a little at a time and stir constantly to produce an even mixture.

4. Bring to the boil and simmer for 15 minutes, uncovered, letting the flavors mingle and the liquid reduce a little. Serve warm or cool with rice or funkaso (*millet pancakes,* p.108) ∎

> **IN ALL RECIPES**
> ● **PEPPER AND SALT ARE TO TASTE.**
> ● **CHILI AND SUGAR ARE GIVEN AS GUIDE QUANTITIES ONLY.**
> **VARY TO TASTE.**
> ● **MEASURES FOR BEANS AND GRAINS REFER TO DRY INGREDIENTS.**

Pay day for women farmworkers, Ghana. *Photo: Bruce Paton/Panos Pictures.*

GHANA

Cowpea/black-eyed bean stew

Serves 4

These creamy-white beans, with their black 'eye' are a staple food in parts of Africa and are also widely eaten in India. Taken to the Americas in the 17th century, the beans are common in the southern United States where they are cooked with rice, hot peppers and (it must be said) salt pork, into the dish called Hopping John.

I N G R E D I E N T S

1 cup / 225 g cowpeas/black-eyed beans, cooked

1 onion, sliced

2 tomatoes, chopped

$^1/_2$ chili, chopped or $^1/_2$ teaspoon chili powder

1-2 tablespoons red palm oil *

salt and pepper

* If you cannot find this, use margarine or cooking oil.

1. Mash the cooked beans and set aside. Heat the oil in a pan and cook the onion and tomatoes a little before adding the mashed beans, chili and seasoning.

2. Let the mixture cook for 10 minutes or so until it combines well. Stir from time to time and add a little water if it becomes too dry. Serve hot with mashed yams, fried plantains or rice ■

Aprapransa (Palm nut stew)

Serves 4

'*Aprapransa* is a delicacy of the Akwapim people (one of the Akan-speaking groups) but it is now eaten by all Ghanaians. It is usually served when a family receives friends or visitors, and then smoked herrings may be added. It uses palm butter, a pulp made from palm nuts, which can sometimes be found in the West in canned form.' *Sophia Twum-Barima, Accra, Ghana*

I N G R E D I E N T S

1 onion, chopped

1 cup / 225 g cowpeas/black-eyed beans, cooked

2-4 tablespoons palm butter or peanut butter *

2 tomatoes, chopped

2 tomatoes, sliced

3 tablespoons corn/maize flour, toasted †

1 tablespoon red palm oil

1 tablespoon lemon juice

water

salt and pepper

* Canned palm butter or palm nut pulp is available in specialist food stores. Peanut butter makes an acceptable alternative.

† To toast the flour, spread it out in a heavy shallow pan and cook it, dry, over a gentle heat until it turns golden.

1. Heat the palm oil in a heavy pan and cook the onion till it is soft. Then add the cooked beans and the palm or peanut butter and a little water as necessary and cook for 5 minutes.

2. Now put in the chopped tomatoes, salt and pepper. Cook for another 5 minutes before tipping in the toasted corn/maize flour; stir well.

3. Pour in the lemon juice, add more water or seasoning if desired and simmer the pot very gently for a further 15 minutes before serving, topped with the tomato slices ■

GHANA

Soy bean and spinach palaver (Stew)

Serves 2-3

'In any vegetarian diet the main meal should include two or more different protein-rich foods (soy beans and pumpkin seeds here) so that any nutritional deficiency in one vegetable protein is made up by the other.' *Charity Kwashie, Accra, Ghana*

Egusie are seeds of an African fruit similar to a pumpkin or gourd. You can substitute pumpkin seeds which are sometimes found in supermarkets as well as in specialist food stores. The nutty flavors of the soy beans and pumpkin seeds complement the spinach perfectly.

I N G R E D I E N T S

1 onion, chopped

3 tomatoes, chopped

$^1/_2$ cup / 50 g egusie or pumpkin seeds

$^1/_4$ cup / 55 g soy beans, cooked

1 pound / 450 g spinach, finely sliced

2 tablespoons red palm oil

salt and pepper

1. First of all, warm the oil in a pan and fry the onion until it turns golden. Now put in the tomatoes and cook them for a few minutes too.

2. While they are cooking, place the egusie or pumpkin seeds in a blender with a little water and make a paste.

3. Now mix the paste into the onion and tomatoes. Stir, and season. Pour in some more water to make a thick sauce and then simmer for 5 minutes or so.

4. When this is ready, put in the cooked soy beans and simmer for another 5-10 minutes. Then place the sliced spinach on top of the sauce, partially cover the pan and cook for 5 minutes.

5. After that, mix the spinach in with the beans and cook over a very low heat for 10 minutes before serving with boiled plantains, yams, potatoes or rice ■

KENYA

Dengu (Green gram/mung beans in coconut milk)

Serves 4

'*Dengu* is the Kiswahili word for green grams or mung beans that are grown by small farmers in the hot and rainy parts of the country. This is a popular dish for people in these areas and is usually served with rice, *chapatis* or sweet potatoes. Today *dengu* is also served in restaurants and is therefore now eaten by many other Kenyans and foreigners.' *Phoebe Omondi, Nairobi, Kenya*

I N G R E D I E N T S

1 cup / 225 g mung dal, cooked *

1 onion, sliced

$^3/_4$ cup / 200 ml coconut milk †

$^1/_4$ teaspoon paprika

slices of red bell pepper

oil

salt

* Mung dal are the hulled, split form of mung beans.

† See p.125.

1. Sprinkle salt to taste on the cooked dal and partially mash with a fork; set aside.

2. Now heat the oil in a heavy pan and sauté the onion till

soft. When it is ready, gradually pour in the coconut milk. Bring the mixture slowly to the boil, stirring well.

3. Next put in the dal and stir so that the ingredients and flavors mingle. Add the paprika and check the seasoning. Garnish with some slices of red bell pepper and serve with rice, phulkas (p.121) or mashed sweet potatoes ■

Nyoyo (Beans and corn)

Serves 4-6

'The basic ingredient of *Nyoyo* is corn/maize and beans which grow in most parts of Kenya. *Nyoyo* is a Luo word for the dish; Kikuyu call it *Githeri*; it is *Muthokoi* for Kambas; *Maenjera* for Luhyas and the Coastal people call it *Pure*. The dish is eaten either for lunch or supper, but the Luo and Luhya also serve it as a snack in the village while doing heavy work such as building a house or farming when other community members come out to help. When cooked without being fried it may also be taken for breakfast with tea or porridge.' *Phoebe Omondi, Nairobi, Kenya*

I N G R E D I E N T S

1 onion, chopped

3 red bell peppers, chopped

4 tomatoes, sliced

1 cup / 225 g cowpeas/black-eyed beans, cooked

2 cups / 300 g corn kernels, cooked or use canned sweet-corn, drained

1 teaspoon paprika

oil

salt and pepper

1. Start by heating the oil in a pan and cooking the onion until it is soft. Then put in the bell peppers and, a little later, the tomatoes.

2. While that is cooking, combine the cooked beans and corn in a bowl and add salt to taste.

3. Now put the corn and bean mixture into the pan containing the onion and tomatoes and season with pepper.

4. Mix well, cover the pot and cook for about 15 minutes or until the ingredients have blended together. Add more water if required during the cooking as the dish should be moist. Serve with rice or bulghur/cracked wheat and a green vegetable or salad ■

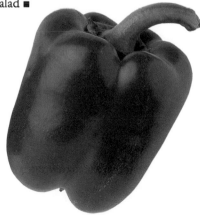

BEANS

In classical Greece and Rome, beans were used for casting votes when electing magistrates and other public officers. When Pythagoras forbade his disciples to have beans, apparently he meant not that they should refrain from eating them but they should not take part in politics. A saucier story has it that beans means sex, so that when Aristotle told his disciples not to eat beans he was not referring to their intake of food.

Whatever the truth of these stories, they show the centrality of beans in the ancient world. Beans, part of the large *leguminosae* family that includes lentils, peas and peanuts, come in a vast array of colours, shapes and sizes. They form the main protein source for vegetarians and people who cannot afford meat all over the world. Many, such as lucerne (alfalfa) are also important forage crops for animals.

One of the best plant-protein beans, soy, is a mainstay for millions of people not just in the form of beans but also as tofu or bean-curd, soy milk and flour and bean sprouts. In the US soy beans are mainly grown to feed intensively-reared animals.

Next to eggs, beans and peas provide vegetarians with the best source of usable protein when combined with cereals and a milk product. Getting to grips with the masses of round, shiny, small, large, speckled, wrinkled, red, white, black, green and yellow varieties is a major challenge, but looking at where they originate is one way to do this.

From Central and South America come the black and red kidney beans, haricots and runner beans, Lima or butter beans and Tepary beans – small protein-packed, mottled beans popular with the Hopi Indians in the south west of the United States, who apparently plant 'three beans for the table, two for the rabbits.'

Africa is the home of the black-eyed bean or cowpea, the pigeon pea or gunga and also the Bambara groundnut. Asia is where soy and azuki beans come from and were first cultivated, probably in China.

From the Indian sub-continent we have chickpeas/garbanzos; black gram (pulse), known as *urad*; green gram known as *mung*; Goa beans; and the small red-brown *moth*, *math* or *moath* beans. When beans, lentils or peas are split they are known as 'dal'. Some are also skinned or hulled. So the green mung bean or green gram becomes 'mung dal' when it is split and hulled to reveal its yellow inside.

The area including the Mediterranean, Middle East and west Asia provided peas, lentils, broad beans, fava beans – and also the locust or carob beans whose uniform shape and weight led to their use as the carat measure for gold.

Many familiar items come from other plants of the *leguminosae* family – Indian hemp; lupins; indigo used for a blue dye; tamarind, an aromatic flavoring; derris insecticide; gum-arabic and tannin from wattle trees, and chewy liquorice ■

KENYA

Irio (Sweetcorn, peas and potato mash)

Serves 4-6

'This is a typical Kikuyu dish from the highlands of Kenya. It is now also served in hotels and restaurants as part of the buffet, alongside international dishes. It is a wholesome meal, tasty and easy to make.' *Phoebe Omondi, Nairobi, Kenya*

Some communities in Kenya share *shambas* or vegetable plots growing corn/maize, groundnuts, root vegetables and *sukuma wiki*, a spinach-like green leafy plant. Planting, hoeing and harvesting are usually done by the women, singing together as they work along the rows.

I N G R E D I E N T S

1 cup / 175 g peas, cooked

2 cups / 300 g corn kernels, cooked or use canned sweet-corn, drained

1/2 pound / 225 g potatoes, chopped and parboiled

1/2 pound / 225 g spinach or greens, cooked

margarine

1 lemon, cut into wedges

salt and pepper

1. Place the peas, corn and potatoes into a bowl. Mash them a little and combine well.

2. Now put the mixture into a saucepan and add the spinach or greens. Warm through over a gentle heat with a little margarine and salt to taste. Serve with a wedge of lemon ■

Kunde (Cowpea/black-eyed bean stew)

Serves 4

'Here is a recipe for vegetarian food commonly used in this part of Africa – served in hotels as well as people's homes. In addition to cowpeas, the women around here also grow cassava, maize and millet. We use the maize and millet to make *ugali*, a porridge that is eaten with stews.' *Juliet Okech, Kisumu, Kenya*

Maize porridge is common in east and southern Africa – it is called *sadza* in Zimbabwe; *oshifima* in Namibia; *mielie-meal* or *putu* in South Africa, and *nshima* in Malawi and Zambia.

I N G R E D I E N T S

1 onion, chopped

6 tomatoes, chopped

1 cup / 225 g cowpeas/black-eyed beans, cooked

1 cup / 125 g peanuts/groundnuts, ground

oil

salt

1. To begin, heat the oil and cook the onion until it turns golden and transparent. Now put in the tomatoes and let them cook for 3 minutes. While they are cooking, mash the beans with a fork.

2. Transfer the beans to the pan containing the onion and tomatoes and cook them also for 5 minutes, stirring from time to time.

3. When this is done, spoon in the ground peanuts and mix them well with the beans and tomatoes. Season and continue to cook gently for 10 minutes before serving with nshima (p.112) or rice ■

from dependence on this crop. Its sights are set on tourism following the publicity from the film *Gorillas in the Mist*, set in Rwanda, about the naturalist Dian Fossey.

INGREDIENTS

1 cup / 225 g pinto, rosecoco or borlotti beans, almost cooked

1/2 pound / 225 g cassava/manioc or potatoes, cut into chunks

4 celery stalks, chopped

1 onion, sliced

oil

salt

1. When the beans are almost cooked, add the cassava/manioc or potato chunks and boil for 10 minutes or so until they are all tender.

2. While that is happening, heat the oil in a pan and cook the onion gently until it turns golden. Add the celery and let it soften.

3. Now drain the beans and cassava/manioc or potatoes and add them to the pan with the onion and celery. Mash the beans and cassava/manioc or potatoes a little, season and mix everything well.

4. Allow the mixture to heat through and blend for 5-10 minutes before serving with a green vegetable and piquant sauce such as kachumbari (p.107) ■

RWANDA

Beans with cassava/manioc

Serves 4-6

Rwanda gained independence from Belgium in 1962 along with its neighbor, Burundi. It has the highest population density in Africa and so far has been able to match the fertility of its people with the fertility of its land to feed the rapidly growing numbers. The staple foods are root crops, especially sweet potatoes.

Coffee is the main export and producer of foreign exchange, but the Government is hoping for a switch away

SOUTH AFRICA

Bean and tomato bredie (Stew)

Serves 2-4

'Dried spotted beans became known as 'Governor's beans' in the Cape – so called because some forgotten governor had planted them in the ample kitchen garden that the Dutch East India Company had first made of the Cape of Good Hope. The beans were always cooked in mutton stock and tomato juice and accompanied by baked pumpkin, flavored with freshly grated nutmeg.

'Here's a vegetarian version. I've not found 'Governor's beans'; in South Africa dried spotted beans are usually called sugar beans, while similar-looking ones in other parts of the world are called pinto or rosecoco beans.' *W. Beinart, Oxford, UK*

I N G R E D I E N T S

2 onions, chopped

2 cloves garlic, chopped

1 tablespoon shallots, leek or chives, chopped

1 teaspoon fresh ginger, grated

2 cardamoms

1 teaspoon fennel seed

pinch of chili powder

1 teaspoon ground coriander

$^1/_2$ cup / 110 g rosecoco, pinto or sugar beans, cooked

1 pound / 450 g tomatoes, chopped

$^1/_2$ pound / 225 g potatoes, cut into large pieces

1 bayleaf

handful fennel leaves +

1 teaspoon thyme, marjoram and/or oregano *

1 teaspoon sugar +

$^1/_2$ glass / 75 ml red wine

$^1/_2$ cup / 50 g raisins, sultanas, dried apricots or other fruit

a little stock or water

oil

salt and pepper

+ optional ingredients

* Fresh herbs are best if you have them.

1. Sauté the onions in the hot oil for a few minutes and when they have begun to soften put in the garlic, shallots, ginger, cardamoms, fennel seed, chili and coriander. Cook for 10 minutes or so, stirring frequently.

2. Now add the beans, tomatoes, potatoes, bayleaf, fennel leaves if using, thyme, marjoram, oregano, sugar if using, wine and the raisins or dried fruit. Season, cover the pot and cook very gently for $1^1/_2$ hours, adding some stock or water as desired, and stirring occasionally ■

Ndebele women cooking porridge for wedding feast, South Africa. *Photo: Margaret Courtney-Clarke.*

TANZANIA

Beans with coconut and cilantro/coriander

Serves 4

The oldest fossils of the human species were found in the Olduvai gorge, in the north of what is now Tanzania, but little is known about the area before the ninth century when the Arab mercantile civilization flourished along the East African coast. Through the centuries after that, the region saw the Portuguese, the Sultans of Oman, the Germans and the British squabbling for control, with the Germans conquering it in the 1890s. After World War One, the region passed to British control. Independence came in 1961, with Zanzibar island joining to form the United Republic of Tanzania in 1964.

I N G R E D I E N T S

3 cloves garlic, crushed

1 green chili, finely chopped or 1 teaspoon chili powder

1 tablespoon ground cumin

1 tablespoon ground coriander

2 teaspoons turmeric

1 tablespoon fresh cilantro/coriander leaves, chopped

1 cup / 75 g dried/desiccated coconut

1 cup / 225 g pinto, rosecoco or cowpeas/black-eyed beans, cooked

1 cup / 175 g potatoes, diced and parboiled

lime or lemon juice to taste

2 tablespoons coconut or other oil

salt

1. Heat the oil and sizzle the garlic together with the chili or chili powder for half a minute.

2. When this is ready, put in the cumin, coriander, turmeric and the cilantro/coriander leaves. Cook for a minute or two, stirring them round to blend. Add the coconut and mix this in too.

3. Now bring in the beans and potatoes; season and then pour the lime or lemon juice over. Cook for 10 minutes or so until everything is blended together and then serve with green vegetables ∎

ZIMBABWE

Nhopi (Corn/maize meal with pumpkin)

Serves 4

'Famed as Zimbabwean ambrosia, celebrated in a song by Oliver Mutukudzi – this is a special dish. It brings a smile to Zimbabweans' lips as "honey" or "strawberries" might to people in the West. *Sadza* or maize meal porridge makes the basis of the dish.' *Yvonne Burgess, Auchtermuchty, UK*

Zimbabwe's near self-sufficiency in food was badly hit by the 1992 drought. But the impact was worsened by the lack of grain stocks – some of which had been sold off partly in response to World Bank pressure on Zimbabwe to reduce its budget deficit.

I N G R E D I E N T S

1 cup / 150 g corn/maize meal

2 cups / 470 ml water

$1/2$ pound / 225 g pumpkin, cooked and mashed (retain cooking water)

$1/2$ teaspoon sugar

2 tablespoons peanut butter

salt

1. Bring the water to the boil and put in the corn/maize meal. Cook, stirring frequently, until it forms a porridge.

2. When it is ready, mix in the mashed pumpkin. Then add the sugar, peanut butter and salt and combine all the ingredients well.

3. Continue to cook for a few minutes, adding about $1/2$ cup/120 ml of the retained pumpkin cooking water if necessary to make the consistency you prefer. Serve immediately with spinach, broccoli or other green vegetable ∎

IN ALL RECIPES
● **PEPPER AND SALT ARE TO TASTE.**
● **CHILI AND SUGAR ARE GIVEN AS GUIDE QUANTITIES ONLY.
VARY TO TASTE.**
● **MEASURES FOR BEANS AND GRAINS REFER TO DRY INGREDIENTS.**

BANGLADESH

Banda kopir tarkari (Vegetables stir-fried with spices)

Serves 4

'In Bangladesh, cabbage is usually available in the market during the winter season, as are tomatoes, peas and carrots. So this dish appears quite frequently at Bengali dinner tables during the winter. In markets where such vegetables are available all year round, *banda* is a popular standard.' *Meghna Guhathakurta, Dhaka, Bangladesh*

I N G R E D I E N T S

$1/2$ teaspoon turmeric

$1/2$ pound / 225 g potatoes, chopped into small cubes

1 onion, finely chopped

1 bayleaf

$1/2$ teaspoon ground cumin

$1/2$ teaspoon ground ginger

$1/4$ teaspoon chili powder

4 tomatoes, chopped

1 cup / 110 g white cabbage, finely sliced

$1/2$ cup / 85 g peas

oil

salt

1. Start by heating the oil in a heavy pan and put in the turmeric and some salt. Fry for a few seconds and then add the cubed potatoes, turning frequently so that they turn yellow from the turmeric. Cook them for 5-10 minutes (they will complete their cooking later) and then remove them from the oil and set aside.

2. Adding more oil if necessary, now sauté the onion slices until they are soft and transparent. Then add the bayleaf, cumin, ginger and chili powder.

3. Stir well and put in the tomatoes. When they have begun to break down, add the cabbage bit by bit, stirring it in well so that it is sautéed in the spices. Cover and cook gently for 3-5 minutes.

4. Finally, put in the peas and semi-fried potatoes and season-ing. Mix well, replace the cover and continue to cook for 5-10 minutes or until the potatoes are ready ■

Labra (Mixed vegetables)

Serves 4

'Although most Bangladeshis are Muslim and non-vegetarian, and even Brahmin (Hindu) priests are allowed to have fish and some meat, there is a trend of vegetarianism in this region which has been strongly influenced by the Vaishnav (from Vishnu, one of the two main Hindu gods) cult of the 16th century.

'The Vaishnav influence in these dishes (which are currently consumed by Hindus of all castes) shows in the absence (*amish*) of meat and fish as well as of pungent flavors such as onion and garlic. Instead, dishes such as *labra* are cooked with a delicate blend of local spices whose aromas mingle with the vegetable being cooked.' *Meghna Guhathakurta, Dhaka, Bangladesh*

I N G R E D I E N T S

$1/2$ teaspoon turmeric

$1/2$ pound / 225 g potatoes, chopped into small cubes

$1/2$ cup / 110 g cauliflower, cut into small pieces

1 teaspoon panch phoron *

1/2 teaspoon fresh ginger, grated

1 cup / 110 g snowpeas/mangetout, sliced into 2 or 3 pieces

1/2 egg-plant/aubergine, cut into small cubes

1 plantain/savory banana, sliced

oil

salt

* Panch phoron or five mixed spices is made up of cumin, fennel, bayleaf, fenugreek and onion seeds. You can buy it ready mixed from Asian stores, or else purchase the individual spices to make your own mix.

1. Taking a heavy pan, heat the oil and sprinkle in the turmeric and salt. Cook them for a few moments and then add the diced potatoes, stirring them into the turmeric mix.

2. After 5 minutes, put in the cauliflower and stir-fry it with the potatoes for another 3 minutes or so, until they are partially cooked and then remove them from the pan and set aside.

3. Now pouring in more oil as necessary, scatter in the panch phoron and let it sizzle until the spices turn brown but do not burn. Then put in the ginger and cook for 1 minute.

4. Next put in the snowpeas/mangetout, egg-plant/aubergine and banana and sauté for 3 minutes before returning the cauliflower and potatoes to the pan.

5. Stir-fry all the ingredients for several minutes and then cover the pan and let it cook slowly for up to 20 minutes or until the potatoes are soft. Season, and stir from time to time. Serve with rice or chapatis ∎

CAMBODIA

Stir-fry with noodles

Serves 4-6

'This is my reconstruction of a delicious Cambodian breakfast dish, which I used to eat when I was in the country making a TV documentary for Oxfam. Onion, chilis and ginger, used in this recipe, are the basis of many Thai-influenced soups and stir-fries in Cambodia, but I have added the carrots. For the chilis, you should use the thumbnail-sized dried ones.'
Julie Christie, London, UK

INGREDIENTS

1 onion, finely sliced

11/2 red chilis, chopped

1 teaspoon fresh ginger, finely chopped

2 cups / 100 g Chinese or ordinary mushrooms, sliced

1/2 pound / 225 g egg noodles

2 carrots, finely sliced

1 cup / 150 g broccoli or cauliflower, chopped

1 cup / 110 g snowpeas/mangetout, cut in half

soy sauce

1-2 tablespoons fresh cilantro/coriander leaves, chopped

oil

1. Prepare the noodles by plunging them into boiling water and then remove the pan from the heat and set aside for 6 minutes, or cook according to the packet instructions.

2. Then heat the oil in the wok and sauté the onion gently for a few minutes until it begins to soften. Put in the chilis and the ginger now and stir-fry these for 2 minutes before adding the mushrooms. These should be sautéed for 2-3 minutes also and then reduce the heat.

3. While that is happening, boil some water in a separate saucepan and cook the carrots, broccoli or cauliflower and snowpeas/mangetout for 3 minutes; drain and then add to the onion mixture. Stir fry for 2-3 minutes, sprinkle on soy sauce to taste, and mix everything well.

4. When they are ready, drain the noodles and scoop them onto a large serving dish. Pile the stir-fry on top, scatter the cilantro/coriander leaves over and serve at once, with additional soy sauce if required ∎

CHINA/HONG KONG

Stir-fry with egg noodles

Serves 4-6

Noodles in Asia come in a variety that makes pasta shells or spaghetti seem quite ordinary. There are buckwheat *soba*; 'cellophane' or 'shining' noodles made of ground mung or soy beans; noodles made of rice flour, potato flour, and seaweed. Egg noodles, made of wheat flour, are long and thin like shoelaces.

As with all stir-fries, the preparation is important so that the ingredients are completely ready when you want to start cooking. For this recipe, fry the bean-curd/tofu first in the wok, and also boil the egg noodles according to the packet instructions.

INGREDIENTS

¹/₄ pound / 110 g egg noodles, cooked

1 cup / 150 g bean-curd/tofu, cubed and fried and/or 2 tablespoons cashew nuts

4 scallions/spring onions, chopped

2 cups / 100 g mushrooms, finely sliced

1 carrot, finely sliced

1 cup / 110 g snowpeas/mangetout

1 cup / 110 g baby sweetcorn

4-6 water chestnuts, sliced +

1 red bell pepper, sliced

1 cup / 50 g bean sprouts

2 tablespoons soy sauce

1-2 tablespoons lemon juice

1 teaspoon fresh ginger, grated

oil

salt

+ optional ingredient

1. To start, heat the oil in a wok or frying pan and cook the scallions/spring onions for a few minutes.

2. Scatter in the mushrooms, carrot, snowpeas/mangetout, baby corn, water chestnuts and red bell pepper and cook these for 2 minutes. Add more oil if necessary.

3. Next put in the bean sprouts and noodles. Mix everything well and then sprinkle in the soy sauce, lemon juice, ginger and salt.

4. When this is done, toss in the bean-curd/tofu and/or cashew nuts. Cook briskly for 1 minute more, with the cover on. Serve right away ∎

INDIA

Dal with coconut

Serves 4

'Dal' in India is a general word meaning pulses which have been skinned and/or halved. Instead of red lentils (*masoor*) you could use the small black beans known as *urad* or the green ones called *mung*, or indeed the unhulled but split versions of these known as *urad* or *mung* dal. Why stop there? You can also try the *moath* bean: a thin, brown bean with a nutty flavor. It's also known as *moth* or *math*, but don't let that put you off.

This is delicious served with boiled rice which has had a handful of raisins and peas thrown into it to cook for the last 5 minutes.

INGREDIENTS

1 cup / 225 g red lentils *

2¹/₂ cups / 590 ml water

¹/₂ teaspoon turmeric

1 teaspoon fresh ginger, chopped coarsely

¹/₂ onion, chopped

3 tablespoons dried/desiccated coconut

1 tablespoon margarine

salt

* If using dal other than red lentils, soak them first for 15 minutes and then cook them until they are just ready.

1. Put the lentils or other dal in a pan and add the water. Bring

to the boil, and remove any froth that rises to the surface.

2. Now add the turmeric, ginger, onion and salt and simmer together for 10 minutes or until the dal is almost done. The water should be almost completely absorbed. Season.

3. At this point, melt the margarine in another pan and stir in the coconut. Cook it gently, stirring, until the coconut turns a rich brown colour.

4. When the dal is ready, spoon it into a serving dish and sprinkle the hot coconut over it ■

Chhole (Garbanzos/chickpeas with tomatoes)

Serves 4

'This is a version of *chhole* that any *Sher-e-Punjab* would be proud of. *Sher-e-Punjab* means "Lion of Punjab", and happens to be the most common name of eating houses owned by Punjabis. *Chhole* is a popular party dish as it is cheap, spicy and flavorsome – especially if you cook it the day before to let the flavors expand.' *Dinyar Godrej, Oxford, UK*

INGREDIENTS

2 onions, thinly sliced

4 cloves garlic, crushed

1-2 green chilis, finely sliced

1 teaspoon turmeric

1 teaspoon paprika

1 tablespoon ground cumin

1 tablespoon ground coriander

1 teaspoon garam masala

4 tomatoes, chopped

2 tablespoons fresh cilantro/coriander leaves, chopped

2 tablespoons fresh mint, chopped or 2 teaspoons dried

1¼ cups / 225 g garbanzos/chickpeas, cooked

oil or ghee

salt and pepper

1. Take a heavy pan and heat the oil or ghee. When it is hot, put in the onions and garlic and sauté them gently for about 5 minutes until golden.

2. Now add the chilis, turmeric, paprika, cumin, ground coriander and garam masala and fry for 2 minutes, stirring frequently.

3. When this is done, put in the tomatoes, 1 tablespoon of the fresh cilantro/coriander leaves together with the mint and cook, stirring, for about 10 minutes until the tomatoes have mushed down to a purée.

4. Put in the garbanzos/chickpeas now and cook for a further 10-15 minutes or better still, remove the pot from the heat and leave for several hours so that the flavors blend well. Then re-heat, scattering the remaining chopped cilantro/coriander leaves on top. Serve with yogurt and cucumber raita or sambal (p.123) ■

Shabnam kari (Curry with peas and mushrooms)

Serves 2-3

Cardamoms, used for this sauce, are the fruits of an Indian plant. They have long been an important spice in south east Asia and the crop is first mentioned in European literature in the 12th century. The delicate spice is used to flavor curries and desserts as well as some liqueurs and the delicious ice-cream *kulfi*. Today, cardamoms are grown commercially in other Asian countries and also in Guatemala. This curry is creamy, not too spicy, and delicious – and it's quick and easy to make. You can use canned mushrooms if you want.

INGREDIENTS

3/4 cup / 110 g frozen or fresh peas

1 onion, finely sliced

2 cloves

1 tablespoon raisins or sultanas

2 cups / 100 g mushrooms, sliced

3 tablespoons cream +

4 tablespoons yogurt

1/2 cup / 120 ml water

2 tablespoons ghee or margarine

handful whole or chopped cashew nuts +

salt

FOR THE PASTE

5 cloves, stalks discarded

1/2 teaspoon fresh ginger, grated

2 tablespoons cashew nuts, chopped

2 tablespoons poppy seeds

seeds from 2 cardamom pods

1 green chili, finely chopped

salt

+ optional ingredients

1. Boil the peas for a few minutes in a little water until they are just tender, then drain them and set aside.

2. While they are cooking, prepare the paste. Put the cloves, ginger, cashew nuts, poppy seeds, cardamom seeds and chili into a blender, adding some water as necessary to give a smooth consistency. Set aside.

3. Returning to the main ingredients, heat the ghee or margarine and sauté the onion until it is soft and golden. Add the cloves and cook for a few moments before spooning in the blended paste, together with the raisins or sultanas. Stir the mixture round while it cooks for 2-3 minutes.

4. After this, add the peas, mushrooms, cream, yogurt and water. Stir well to amalgamate and season with salt. Cook gently for 5 minutes before serving with the cashew nuts scattered on top ■

Tamarind dal

Serves 2-4

Tamarind, from *tamar-i-hind*, 'the date of the East', is thought to be indigenous to Africa but was introduced into India in pre-historic times. The trees live for over 100 years and need little active managing. The pulp around the seeds gives dishes an intriguing sourness, and the seeds yield a glue as well as pectin and tartaric acid. Tamarind wood is hard and makes good charcoal: useful for the many cooking stoves in India's villages. You could make this recipe also using *toor dal* (from pigeon peas), *urad dal* (from a small black bean) or *mung dal* (from the mung bean).

INGREDIENTS

1 tablespoon / 50 g tamarind pulp, soaked in 1/2 cup / 120 ml warm water for 20 minutes

1 teaspoon cumin seeds

1 green chili, chopped

1 teaspoon fresh ginger, finely chopped

1/2 teaspoon chili powder

2 teaspoons garam masala

2 tablespoons fresh cilantro/coriander leaves, chopped

1/2 cup / 110 g red lentils, cooked

oil

salt

1. When the tamarind has soaked for 20 minutes, place it in a sieve above the bowl containing the water it was soaked in

and press the pulp through. Mix well with the water and set aside.

2. Heat a pan without oil and then toast the cumin seeds in it, stirring frequently until they turn a darker color. Then transfer them to a bowl or mortar and crush them.

3. Now add the chili, ginger, chili powder, garam masala, cumin seeds, cilantro/coriander leaves and a little salt to the bowl containing the tamarind water. Stir well and leave to stand for 15 minutes.

4. While that is happening, heat up some oil in a pan and fry the lentils or other dal over a brisk heat for 5 minutes. After that, pour in the tamarind mixture and continue to simmer for 5-10 minutes, stirring to distribute the spicy sauce. Serve with rice or phulkas (see p.121) ■

Dhansak (Lentil purée)

Serves 4

A typical *Parsi* dish – lentil purée supplemented with vegetables. *Parsis* are Zoroastrians, a religion founded on the life of Zoroaster in Persia from 630-553 BC. After his death the religion spread all over Persia until the Muslim invasion forced the remaining *Parsis* down into India.

The *Parsis* are a small but enterprising community in India; their cuisine tends towards meat and fish, their conception of vegetables being lentils, potatoes and also eggs. The captivating taste of *dhansak* gives a glimpse of their culinary flair.

1 teaspoon cumin seeds
1 teaspoon mustard seeds
1 stick cinnamon
6 green cardamom pods
1 onion, finely chopped
2 cloves garlic, crushed
1 carrot, thinly sliced
3-4 tomatoes, chopped
1 red or green bell pepper, chopped
1 cup / 225 g toor dal or red lentils, cooked
1 tablespoon mild curry powder
$^{1}/_{2}$ cup / 120 ml coconut milk
4 tablespoons fresh cilantro/coriander leaves, chopped
2 tablespoons fresh mint, chopped or 2 teaspoons dried
1 cup / 150 g paneer cheese, cubed and fried [*]
2 tablespoons cashew nuts
a squeeze of lemon juice
oil
salt

* This curd cheese (obtainable in Asian stores) is rather similar to bean-curd/tofu in that it absorbs surrounding aromas while providing protein. You can omit it and serve the dish with yogurt instead.

1. First heat the oil in a wok or large pan and then put in the cumin seeds, mustard seeds, cinnamon and cardamoms. Stir-fry them for a few moments before adding the onion, garlic and carrot. Then cook these, stirring all the time, for 3-4 minutes.

2. Next add the tomatoes and bell pepper and simmer for 10 minutes. When this is done, spoon in the lentils. Mix in the curry powder, coconut milk, cilantro/coriander leaves, mint and salt.

3. Stir well to combine all the ingredients and then add the paneer, if using, as well as the cashew nuts. Squeeze in some lemon juice to taste and continue to cook gently for a further 10 minutes, stirring so that it does not stick. Add a little water or more coconut milk if necessary ■

MALAYSIA

Coconut curry with peanut sauce

Serves 2-4

'Malaysia being multi-ethnic – Indian, Chinese and Malay – produces some lovely food in the markets, a mixture of everything. This is my attempt to duplicate those delicious coconut curries I ate there. They can be made using fish but you could substitute hard-boiled eggs or chunks of fried bean-curd/tofu.'
Julie Christie, London, UK

I N G R E D I E N T S

1 cup / 150 g bean-curd/tofu, cut into 1-inch/2.5-cm chunks or 4 hard-boiled eggs

1 cup / 225 g rice

1 onion, sliced

1/3 brick of creamed coconut *

1 tablespoon tomato paste

2 tablespoons peanut butter

1/2 teaspoon curry powder

1/2 teaspoon chili powder +

squeeze of lemon or lime

margarine or oil

salt

* Available in some supermarkets as well as in most Asian stores.

+ optional ingredients

1. If using bean-curd/tofu instead of eggs, heat a little oil in a wok and briskly stir-fry the bean-curd/tofu for a few minutes until the chunks are golden on all sides. Then remove them, drain, and set aside.

2. Next take a large saucepan and melt a little margarine in it, or warm some oil. Tip in the rice and turn it around as it heats until it is translucent. Then pour on boiling water to cover the rice by about 1 inch/2.5 cms. Put the lid on and simmer for 20 minutes or until the water has all been absorbed and the rice is just soft.

3. While that is cooking, place the creamed coconut in a wok over a moderate heat: it will quickly break down and needs water adding from time to time to stop it burning. Place the onion in the coconut cream and let it cook gently for 3 minutes or so.

4. Now spoon in the tomato purée and peanut butter. Stir, and as the mixture begins to coagulate and become dry add a little more water to make a thick but liquid paste.

5. Shake in the curry powder, and chili powder if using, and mix in. Taste: coconut should be the dominant flavor, with peanut next. Add more coconut if required and keep the mixture moist with water until you have a creamy sauce.

6. When ready, spoon the rice on a serving plate, arrange the eggs or bean-curd/tofu pieces on top and pour the sauce over. Add a squeeze of lemon or lime juice for extra zest ∎

Gado-gado (Cooked vegetable salad with peanut sauce)

Serves 6

Malaysia's cities are clean, tranquil and friendly and the economy is thriving. Tourists flock to the beautiful beaches and enjoy the wonderful food. But the country is blemished by intolerance for trade unionists, environmentalists and others seeking social justice.

Coconut milk (see p.125), used in this recipe, is a favorite in south east Asian cooking. The coconut palm is among 2,600 species of palm trees which are amazingly versatile in their uses providing building materials, food, fuel, oil and wax.

I N G R E D I E N T S

1 cup / 150 g bean-curd/tofu, sliced

1 cup / 50 g bean sprouts

1 cup / 110 g snowpeas/mangetout or other green beans, sliced into 1-inch/2.5-cm lengths

1 potato, sliced and cooked

6 inches / 15 cms cucumber, grated or cut into fine sticks

1 cup / 110 g cabbage, shredded

1 cup / 50 g lettuce, cut finely

3 eggs, hardboiled and sliced +

oil

FOR THE SAUCE

2 cups / 225 g peanuts, roasted and ground *

1 stalk lemon grass or 1 teaspoon lemon juice †

2 chilis, sliced finely

1 clove garlic, crushed

5 shallots, chopped

2 tablespoons sugar

1 tablespoon lemon or lime juice

1 cup / 240 ml coconut milk

salt

+ optional ingredient

* Or use $^1/_2$ cup / 110 g peanut butter.

† Lemon grass can be found in health food stores or Chinese supermarkets. You can also find dried, packaged lemon grass.

1. First heat the oil and fry the slices of bean-curd/tofu until they are golden. Drain on kitchen paper and set aside.

2. Now boil some water in a saucepan or use a steamer and lightly cook the bean sprouts, snowpeas/mangetout and cabbage, until they are just done.

3. Arrange the vegetables together with the potato, cucumber, lettuce and hardboiled eggs decoratively on a serving dish, leaving room in the center for a bowl containing the peanut sauce.

4. To make the sauce, pound or blend the lemon grass or lemon juice with the chilis, garlic and shallots.

5. Then heat some oil in a wok or fry pan and gently sauté these ingredients for 2 minutes. Add the sugar, salt, lemon or lime juice and coconut milk. Simmer, uncovered, for about 10 minutes.

6. When this is ready, spoon in the ground peanuts or peanut butter to make a thick sauce. Adjust to taste by adding more lemon juice, salt, sugar or coconut milk as liked. To serve, people take a mixture of vegetables and spoon the hot sauce over ■

Tauhu goreng (Filled bean-curd/tofu cakes with spicy peanut sauce)

Serves 4

Malaysia's cuisine is rich and varied, drawing on the three main population groups – Malays, Chinese and Indians. Here the typically Malay and Indonesian chili-and-peanut sauce accompanies (Chinese) bean-curd/tofu cakes. 'Firm' tofu is best for these bean-curd/tofu 'sandwiches'.

I N G R E D I E N T S

4 bean-curd/tofu cakes

1 cup / 50 g bean sprouts, scalded

3 inches / 7.5 cms cucumber, shredded

salt

oil

FOR THE SAUCE

2 green chilis, sliced

2 red chilis, sliced

2 cloves garlic, crushed

1¹/₂ tablespoons soy sauce

1¹/₂ tablespoons vinegar

2 cups / 225 g peanuts, roasted
   and pounded/blended *

³/₄ cup / 200 ml water

2 tablespoons fresh cilantro/coriander leaves, chopped

salt

* Or substitute ¹/₂ cup / 110 g peanut butter.

1. Heat enough oil (about 2 inches/5 cms deep) in a wok or pan to deep-fry the bean-curd/tofu cakes until they are slightly brown. Lift them out and let them cool.

2. Then cut each cake into 2 pieces and make a deep slit across the center to form a pocket.

3. After that, mix the bean sprouts and cucumber in a bowl and season well before filling the bean-curd/tofu pouches.

4. For the sauce, pound or blend the chilis and garlic together. Then add the soy sauce, vinegar and salt. Next put in the ground peanuts and add the water a little at a time. Stir to

make a smooth coating sauce.

5. Arrange the stuffed bean-curd/tofu cakes on a dish; garnish with slices of cucumber and fresh cilantro/coriander leaves and pass the peanut sauce separately ∎

NEPAL

Dal-bhaat and tarkari (Lentils and curried vegetables)

Serves 4

'This is the main Nepali meal. In the villages, rice is served only to guests or on festival occasions. Instead, a heavy porridge is made from maize, millet or wheat flour boiled in water. The lentils or the vegetables are often omitted and a single accompanying sauce called *tyun* is made from whatever dried beans or vegetables are available – such as stinging nettle and fern shoots. Very little oil is used and the main spicing is from chilis and salt.' *Joy Stephens, Kathmandu, Nepal*

I N G R E D I E N T S

FOR THE DAL

1 onion, chopped

2 cloves garlic, crushed

¹/₄ teaspoon fresh ginger, grated

¹/₂ teaspoon turmeric

1 cup / 225 g red lentils

oil

salt

FOR THE CURRIED VEGETABLES

1 pound / 450 g mixed vegetables, chopped (potatoes, carrots, peas or whatever you have to hand) *

¹/₂ green chili, finely chopped or ¹/₂ teaspoon chili powder

¹/₄ teaspoon fresh ginger, grated

1 teaspoon ground coriander

1 teaspoon ground cumin

oil

salt

* If you are using root vegetables and/or cauliflower, parboil them first for 5 minutes.

1. For the dal, heat up some oil in a saucepan and then sauté the onion for a few minutes followed by the garlic until both

ingredients are soft but not browned. Now add the ginger and cook this too for a minute or so.

2. Next, put in the lentils and the turmeric and stir them round so that they combine with the onion, garlic and ginger.

3. When this is done, pour on enough water to submerge the lentils, cover the pot, and bring to the boil. Then reduce the heat and simmer for about 20 minutes or until the lentils are soft and have absorbed most of the water. Season and keep warm in a serving bowl.

4. While that is cooking, prepare the curried vegetables. Take a large pan, heat the oil and fry the chili or chili powder, the ginger, coriander, cumin and salt. Cook this mixture for a few minutes, stirring frequently.

5. When you have done this, put in the vegetables and turn them around in the pan so that they are well coated with the spices. Add a little water and then cook them for 10-20 minutes (depending on which ones you are using) until they are ready. Serve the lentils and vegetables in separate dishes, with rice ■

PAKISTAN

Rajma (Red kidney beans in sauce)

Serves 2-3

The poet-philosopher Mohammad Iqbal articulated the concept of Pakistan in 1931 when he proposed a separate state for the Muslims in India. This 'partition' of the subcontinent upon independence from Britain in 1947 led to Pakistan's birth as a nation: 'Pakistan – the land of the pure'.

INGREDIENTS

1 cup / 225 g red kidney beans, cooked (retain the cooking water)

1 teaspoon cumin seeds

1 onion, sliced thinly

2 cloves garlic, crushed

$^1/_2$ teaspoon fresh ginger, grated

1 green chili, chopped finely

$^1/_2$ teaspoon garam masala

1 teaspoon ground coriander

$^1/_2$ teaspoon turmeric

3-4 tomatoes or 1 can tomatoes

sugar to taste +

1 tablespoon fresh cilantro/coriander leaves, chopped

oil

salt

+ optional ingredient

1. Begin by heating the oil and then fry the cumin seeds until they begin to jump about and turn a shade darker. Add the onion, garlic, ginger and chopped chili. Stirring all the time, cook the mixture for a few minutes to combine the flavors.

2. The garam masala, ground coriander and turmeric go in next. Stir well and continue frying for a few minutes. After that, put in the tomatoes and let the mixture cook for 5 minutes, stirring from time to time.

3. While that is cooking, prepare the cooked beans. Drain them if you have not already done so. Take out about half and mash with a fork; then return them to the pan.

4. Spoon the tomato and spice mixture into the beans and combine all the ingredients well. If the stew looks too dry, add some of the retained bean water.

5. Bring the pan to the boil over a gentle heat and season the mixture, adding sugar if using. Cook it for 10-20 minutes to let the flavors blend and then serve with the fresh cilantro/coriander leaves scattered on top ■

Making charcoal, Sri Lanka. *Photo: Sally and Richard Greenhill.*

SRI LANKA

Cadju curry (Cashew nut curry)

Serves 4

'The main cooking utensils used in Sri Lanka are clay *chatties* or pots which give curries a special flavor (but an ordinary saucepan will do). Though many city homes use electricity and gas, traditional Lankan cooking is done on the age-old wood-fuelled hearth made of three stones kept apart as a tri-angle, the cooking vessel balancing on the stones and the fuel-wood firing the cooking. There are special stone grinders, and pestles and mortars for pounding rice and spices – with elec-tric blenders increasingly used.

"Curry" means sauce – and here is a favorite one using *cadju* (cashew) nuts. This is delicious with *chapatis*, noodles or rice.' *Mavis and Nalin Wijesekera, Mount Lavinia, Sri Lanka*

I N G R E D I E N T S

1 cinnamon stick

1 clove

1 cardamom pod

3-4 curry leaves or 1 stalk lemon grass *

1/2 onion, finely sliced

3 cloves garlic, crushed

1 teaspoon fenugreek seeds, crushed †

2 teaspoons ground coriander

1 teaspoon ground cumin

1 teaspoon chili powder

1/4 teaspoon turmeric

2 cups / 250 g cashew nuts

1³/4 cups / 420 ml coconut milk

oil

salt

* Lemon grass can be found in health food stores or Chinese supermarkets. You can also find dried, packaged lemon grass.

† Fenugreek seeds are hard to crush, but it is possible. You may prefer to use ground fenugreek.

1. First heat the oil in a heavy pan and fry the cinnamon, clove, cardamom and curry leaves or lemon grass for a few moments before adding the onion and garlic.

2. The ground fenugreek seeds, coriander, cumin, chili, turmeric and cashews go in now; stir well.

3. Let everything cook together for 5 minutes to combine well. Then slowly pour in the coconut milk and stir round. Season, and simmer gently for 10 minutes before serving with boiled rice into which a few raisins or sultanas have been thrown while cooking ■

> **IN ALL RECIPES**
> ● **PEPPER AND SALT ARE TO TASTE.**
> ● **CHILI AND SUGAR ARE GIVEN AS GUIDE QUANTITIES ONLY.**
> **VARY TO TASTE.**
> ● **MEASURES FOR BEANS AND GRAINS REFER TO DRY INGREDIENTS.**

ARGENTINA

Empanadas (Turnovers)

Serves 4-6

The vast *pampas* of central Argentina, with their fertile soil and favorable climate, is where the country's agricultural exports are grown. Crops are beginning to replace beef production, with wheat, corn/maize, sorghum, soy, rice, sugarcane and grapes among the produce. Argentina is the world's third major producer of soy beans, and the fifth largest wine producer.

These tasty pasties or turnovers can be made with a variety of fillings. Instead of peaches, try mango or dried apricots.

I N G R E D I E N T S

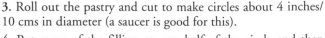

$1/2$ pound / 225 g frozen flaky pastry, thawed

1 onion, finely chopped

2 tomatoes, chopped

1 green bell pepper, finely chopped

1 tablespoon chives, chopped

1 pear, finely sliced

2 peaches, finely sliced

$1/2$ cup / 110 g red lentils, cooked

1 tablespoon sugar +

$1/4$ cup / 60 ml dry white wine +

$1/2$ teaspoon cinnamon

2 tablespoons margarine

salt and pepper

+ optional ingredients

Heat oven to 400°F/200°C/Gas 6

1. To begin, heat the margarine in a heavy pan and fry the onion until it is soft. Then put in the tomatoes, bell pepper and chives; stir, and cook for 5 minutes or so.

2. Now add the pear, peaches, and lentils and mix well. Sprinkle in some sugar if using and pour in wine to taste. Add a little cinnamon and then season.

3. Roll out the pastry and cut to make circles about 4 inches/ 10 cms in diameter (a saucer is good for this).

4. Put some of the filling on one half of the circle and then moisten the edges with a little water. Fold over the other half and press the two sides together with the back of a fork. Make a couple of punctures in the top of the turnover to let the steam escape.

5. Fill the other empanadas in the same way and then place them on a baking tray in the oven for about 20 minutes until the pastry is puffed up and golden. Serve at once with a green salad ∎

BAHAMAS

Gunga (Pigeon peas and rice)

Serves 6-8

'The Arawaks (Indians) turned their hearts to us,' wrote Columbus on arrival in the Bahamas in 1492, *'we have become such great friends.'* But alas that friendship was one-sided: the Spanish were soon busily rounding up the Arawaks and shipping them to Spain as slaves.

Despite the Bahamas' subtropical climate, the lack of rivers has limited commercial cropping to sisal and cotton; tourism is the main source of foreign exchange.

I N G R E D I E N T S

1 onion, chopped

1 green bell pepper, chopped

2 tablespoons tomato paste

1 can tomatoes, drained (keep the juice)

$1/2$ tablespoon fresh thyme, chopped or 1 teaspoon dried

1 cup / 225 g pigeon peas, cooked until almost tender

1 cup / 225 g rice

$1/2$ lemon

oil

salt and pepper

1. Sauté the onion and bell pepper in the oil until they are soft. Then put in the tomato paste, the tomatoes and thyme.

Chop or mash the tomatoes and stir; season and then cook the mixture for 5 minutes.

2. After this, add the pigeon peas and the juice from the tomatoes. Sprinkle in the rice and add enough water to cover it by approximately $1/2$ inch/1.5 cms.

3. Stir, and then bring the pan to the boil. Now reduce the heat, cover, and cook the rice for 20–30 minutes, stirring from time to time. Serve hot with a squeeze of lemon ■

BOLIVIA

Locro (Squash/pumpkin stew)

Serves 6

'This stew is a favorite Bolivian recipe and comes from the Cochabamba Valley. The squash used is a big yellow variety (as large as a pumpkin) with a green exterior, but you can make it with most of the small yellow squashes. The cheese it uses is *quesillo*, a homemade farmers' cheese which is salty and crumbly – similar to Greek *feta*.

'*Habas* are an Andean broad bean and *chochlo* is the type of corn with large, pale yellow kernels found in the Andes region.' *Reina Ayala and Linda Farthing, Cochabamba, Bolivia*

I N G R E D I E N T S

2 pounds / 1 kg squash, pumpkin or sweet potato, peeled and cut into 1-inch/2.5-cm chunks

$1/2$ cup / 120 ml water

1 onion, chopped

1 tomato, chopped

$1/2$ teaspoon oregano

1-2 cobs of corn, cut into 2-inch/5-cm pieces *

1 pound / 450 g potatoes, cut into cubes and parboiled

$1/2$ cup / 85 g habas, butter beans or Lima beans, cooked

$1/2$ cup / 85 g peas

1 cup / 100 g feta or other crumbly cheese

1 tablespoon fresh parsley, chopped

oil

salt and pepper

* You can also use baby sweetcorn or canned sweetcorn.

1. Put the water into a pan with the squash, pumpkin or sweet potato and bring it to the boil; cook until it begins to soften.

2. While that is happening, heat the oil in another pan and sauté the onion and then add the tomato, oregano and salt and pepper. Put this mixture into the squash and combine well.

3. The corn, potatoes and beans go in now. Let them cook gently in the squash stew for 10 minutes or so and then add the peas.

4. When the corn is cooked, crumble in the cheese or cut it into cubes and add these. Heat through and stir carefully until the cheese begins to melt. Now cast the chopped parsley on top and serve right away ■

'Moors and Christians' – apparently referring to the black beans (Moors) and white rice (Christians).

INGREDIENTS

2 cups / 450 g black or red kidney beans, cooked

1/4 teaspoon chili powder

1 onion, chopped finely

1 cup / 100 g grated cheese

3 tomatoes, chopped

1/2 teaspoon fresh basil or parsley, chopped

oil

salt and pepper

1. Place the beans in a bowl and mash them with a fork, or use a blender. Sprinkle on the chili powder, season and mix well again.

2. Then heat the oil and cook the onion so that it softens. Add the bean mash and fry it over a gentle heat, stirring all the time, until it has a firm consistency.

3. Transfer the beans to a serving dish, scatter the grated cheese over and keep hot.

4. Now make a sauce by placing the chopped tomatoes, basil or parsley, seasoning, and a little water if necessary and chili powder if liked, into a saucepan or blender and mix well. Heat it up and serve alongside the frijoles together with rice or corn chips/nachos ∎

BRAZIL

Frijoles refritos (Fried beans)

Serves 4-6

Fried beans is one of the region's most popular dishes; fortunately it is nutritious too. In Central America it is often complemented by corn/maize *tortillas* (corn/maize pancakes), and with the addition of scrambled egg, it is an anytime food.

In Brazil, *frijoles* are usually made with black beans and served with rice. A Caribbean version of this dish is called

CHILE

Porotos (Bean and pumpkin stew)

Serves 4

'I came to live in Britain about two years ago when I was 12. It is very different here than in Chile so my father and I like to eat Chilean food to remind us of home. Beans are called *porotos* in Chile, and this dish is a popular meal for us – we eat it with spaghetti like we did in Viña del Mar.' *Paula Pigot, Oxford, UK*

I N G R E D I E N T S

1 onion, sliced

2 cloves garlic, crushed

$1/2$ teaspoon chili powder

$1/2$ teaspoon cumin seeds

4-6 tomatoes, chopped

1 cup / 225 g white kidney or flageolet beans, cooked

1 pound / 450 g pumpkin, cubed and cooked (retain the cooking water) *

$1/2$ pound / 225 g spaghetti

1 tablespoon fresh basil, chopped

oil

salt and pepper

* Or use sweet potato.

1. First, heat the oil and gently fry the onion until it is soft and transparent. Then put in the garlic, chili powder and cumin seeds and cook for a couple of minutes before adding the chopped tomatoes.

2. When the tomatoes have softened, the beans and pumpkin can be added together with some of the pumpkin water if you wish. Season, cover, and leave to stew for a few minutes while you cook the spaghetti in boiling water according to the packet instructions.

3. Once the pasta is ready, drain it and then transfer to a serving dish or spoon it onto plates and ladle the stew over. Garnish with the fresh basil ∎

COLOMBIA

Ochos rios (Coconut rice and beans)

Serves 4

Site of the ancient Chibchan culture, Colombia was colonized by the Spanish in the 1550s and over the next 300 years its indigenous population all but disappeared. The main exports are coffee, processed coca (cocaine) and bananas and Colombia also has plentiful mineral resources such as oil, coal and gold.

I N G R E D I E N T S

1 onion, sliced

$1/2$ cup / 120 ml stock

$1/2$ chili, seeded and finely chopped

$1/2$ teaspoon thyme

$1/2$ cup / 110 g rice, cooked

$1/2$ cup / 110 g kidney beans, cooked

1 cup / 75 g dried/desiccated coconut

2-3 tablespoons milk

oil

salt

1. To begin, sauté the onion in the heated oil and then put in the stock, chili, thyme and a little salt. Cover and bring to the boil.

2. Now add the cooked beans and rice, followed by the coconut. Stir well and then let the mixture simmer, uncovered, for about 20 minutes so that the ingredients and flavors blend well.

3. After this, stir in the milk and heat the mixture through gently before serving accompanied by a green salad and/or chutney ∎

IN ALL RECIPES
● **PEPPER AND SALT ARE TO TASTE.**
● **CHILI AND SUGAR ARE GIVEN AS GUIDE QUANTITIES ONLY.**
VARY TO TASTE.
● **MEASURES FOR BEANS AND GRAINS REFER TO DRY INGREDIENTS.**

Indian woman cooking on outdoor stove, Peru. *Photo: Maximilien Bruggmann.*

1. To begin, melt the margarine and cook the onions until they are soft and golden.

2. Transfer them to a bowl when ready and combine them with the mashed potatoes, parsley and cheese, adding salt and pepper to taste.

3. Now shape this potato mixture into cakes about 1 inch/ 2.5 cm thick. Heat a little oil in a frying pan or use a griddle. When it is very hot, cook the cakes until they are golden on one side and then turn them over to brown the other side. Keep the potato cakes warm while you prepare the rest of the dish as below.

4. Spoon the peanut butter into a small saucepan and add the stock, stirring well so that it is evenly absorbed. Heat gently.

5. While that is happening, poach the eggs in a little water. To serve, place the potato cakes on a dish lined with lettuce leaves, slide the eggs on top and pass the peanut sauce round separately ■

ECUADOR

Llapingachos (Potato cakes with peanut sauce)

Serves 6

The Equator runs through Ecuador, and if you follow its line westwards you reach Ecuador's other territory, the Galapagos Islands. This, you will remember, is where Charles Darwin put the nuts and bolts on his theory of evolution as he described related but different species of plants and animals on the islands.

This dish brings together some of Ecuador's staple foods – potatoes, eggs and peanuts into a favorite dish.

I N G R E D I E N T S

2 onions, finely chopped

2 pounds / 1 kg potatoes, mashed

2 tablespoons fresh parsley, chopped

2 cups / 200 g cheddar or monterrey jack cheese, grated

1/2 cup / 110 g peanut butter

1/2 cup / 120 ml stock or water

6 eggs

lemon juice

a few lettuce leaves

2 tablespoons margarine

oil

salt and pepper

HAITI

Aubergines en peau (Stuffed egg-plant/aubergine)

Serves 4

Haiti was the home of the early 19th century slave revolt leader, François Toussaint, whose forces repelled the Spanish, British and French. Toussaint was captured and he died in a French gaol, while his generals continued the struggle which led to Haiti's independence as the world's first black republic in 1804. But the country's recent history, under the dictatorial Duvalier family, has been pitiful. Later attempts at democracy have been halting, with elected President Aristide quickly bundled out of office and into exile.

This dish is simple, and makes a pleasant light meal on its own or with a salad.

INGREDIENTS

2 egg-plants/aubergines, halved lengthwise

1 onion, chopped

2 slices bread, diced, and soaked in 1 cup/240 ml milk

1 egg

2 cups / 200 g monterrey jack or cheddar cheese, grated

2 heaped tablespoons breadcrumbs or sesame seeds

oil

salt and pepper

Heat oven to 350°F/180°C/Gas 4

1. Start by boiling the egg-plant/aubergine halves in a little water, turning once, for 5 minutes or so. Drain. When they are cool, remove the pulp with a spoon and cut it into small chunks. Keep the egg-plant/aubergine shells.

2. Now heat the oil in a pan and cook the onion until it is soft; then add the egg-plant/aubergine pieces and cook these together for about 5 minutes.

3. After this, squeeze the bread and put it into the onion mixture, adding salt and pepper to taste. Mix the ingredients together well and then remove the pan from the heat.

4. Beat the egg in a small bowl and then pour it into the pan containing the onion and egg-plant/aubergine mix. Add half the cheese and mix everything together well.

5. Now place the egg-plant/aubergine shells on a greased oven-proof dish and then pile the mixture into them. Top with the remaining cheese and scatter the breadcrumbs or sesame seeds over. Bake for 15-20 minutes ■

MEXICO

Molletes

Serves 4

'*Molletes* is usually eaten in Mexico as a light supper in the evening. But with the additions of a *guacamole* starter (p.56), some relish, (p.130), salad (p.129) and dessert (p.155), we think it makes a superb meal.' *Caitlin Buck and José Andrés Christen, Leeds, UK, and Mexico*

There are about 100 types of chili, fresh or dried, with colors ranging from pale green to almost black. One of the most common are *jalepeños*. You will always find a chili sauce or *salsa* on the table when you eat, and this may be home-made. Chili is also the basis of the cooked sauce *mole*, a tongue-tickling mixture of chocolate, chili and up to 50 other ingredients.

INGREDIENTS

1 stick of French bread

1 cup / 225 g black or red kidney beans, cooked

$^1/_2$ pound / 225 g cheddar or monterrey jack cheese, grated

$^1/_4$ chili, chopped finely or $^1/_2$ teaspoon chili powder

water

oil

salt and pepper

Heat oven to 350°F/180°C/Gas 4

1. First slice the French bread into 4 sections and then slice each piece in half lengthwise. Scoop out some of the bread from each piece to make 8 'boats' or cradles which will later be filled with beans.

2. Place the beans in a bowl, add the chili powder, the salt and pepper and also a little water. Partially mash the beans with a fork, potato masher or use a blender.

3. Next, heat up the oil in a large pan and when it is very hot, fry the mashed beans to make frijoles refritos (refried beans). You may need to do this in more than one batch unless the pan is very large.

4. When the beans are ready, fill the hollows in the bread with the mixture and top with the grated cheese.

5. Place the bread sections on a baking tray and cook in the oven until they have heated through and the cheese is golden on top. Serve with the relish, pico de gallo (p.130) and berros salad (p.129) on the side ∎

LENTILS

REMEMBER Jacob and Esau, the biblical twins, one hairy, one not? And how Esau, the first-born child, sold his birthright to Jacob for a mess of pottage. What you may not have realized was that the pottage was made of red lentils.

Lentils, the small round seeds of a pea-like plant, have been cultivated since the earliest days of settled farming. Almost 8,000 years ago in the rich 'fertile crescent' between the rivers Tigris and Euphrates, in what is now Iraq and Syria, the Sumerians were growing lentils, beans and chickpeas along with cereals such as wheat and vegetables including onions, leeks and lettuce. St Augustine wrote that 'lentils are used as a food in Egypt, for this plant grows abundantly in that country, which renders the lentils of Alexandria (in Egypt) so valuable that they are brought from thence to us, as if we grew none.'

Lentils were an important component of the expanding Mediterranean agriculture, providing a major source of protein in the region, particularly for poorer people. The Hebrew word for lentils, *adashim*, comes from *adeesh* meaning 'to tend a flock' – indicating perhaps that it was food for peasants and herders.

In Europe, from the 11th century onwards, a common food was dumplings cooked in the cauldron – and often they were made from dried legumes: pease pudding is an example. Elsewhere, in India for instance, lentils were widely cultivated nearly 2,000 years ago, along with peas, beans, and gourds. Early curries contained many of the distinctive ingredients still used today such as onions, lentils or dal cooked in ghee (clarified butter) and flavored with cardamom, cumin, coriander and turmeric.

The split red lentils found in every supermarket are just one of a colourful range of this branch of the *leguminosae* family. These come from the Egyptian or Syrian brown lentils which have been split and hulled. As split red lentils, they need no soaking, are quick to cook and mash down into a congenial thick soupy consistency when ready. Then there are the larger green European and the grey Puy variety which take a little longer to cook but retain their shape.

Lentils are one of the most tasty and nutritious pulses. With their protein content they are important meat substitutes in many peasant communities, and among other people wishing to omit animal flesh from their diet.

France is the world's largest exporter of all pulses (beans, peas, lentils but excluding peanuts), followed by the US and then China ∎

Avocado and zucchini/courgette enchiladas (Filled pancakes)

Serves 3-4

The cultures of Mexico – Olmeca, Teotihuacan, Maya and Mexica – have made outstanding contributions in art, science and technology as well as in political and social organization. This legacy was evident in the wealth and sophistication of Aztec emperor Montezuma's city, Tenochtitlan. It certainly dazzled the Spaniards when they arrived in the 15th century. Today, Mexico City is still breath-taking but for different reasons. It is one of the largest metropolises in the world, along with Shanghai, Tokyo and New York – and also one of the most polluted.

Try making these *enchiladas* with other fillings – sweetcorn, tomato and bell peppers for instance – and serve them all together. Instead of the *guacamole* (avocado pear) topping you could use more cheese.

INGREDIENTS

FOR THE GUACAMOLE TOPPING

1 avocado pear

1 clove garlic, crushed

$1/2$ teaspoon chili, seeded and finely chopped

juice of $1/2$ lime or lemon

1-2 tomatoes, sliced, for garnish

salt and pepper

8-12 ready-made taco shells or tortillas, or see recipe p.128

FOR THE FILLING

$1/2$ onion, finely chopped

1 clove garlic, crushed

$1/2$ chili, finely sliced

2 zucchini/courgettes, sliced

1 green bell pepper, chopped

2 tablespoons walnuts, chopped

$1/2$ teaspoon cinnamon

3 cups / 300 g monterrey jack or cheddar cheese, grated

oil

salt and pepper

Heat oven to 325°F/160°C/Gas 3

1. First, make the guacamole by cutting the avocado pear in half and scooping the flesh with a teaspoon into a bowl. Then mash it with a fork, add the garlic, chili and lime juice. Season.

2. For the filling, heat the oil in a frying pan and sauté the onion. When it is ready, add the garlic, chili, zucchini/courgettes, bell pepper and chopped walnuts.

3. Cook for 5-10 minutes until the vegetables are soft and the ingredients have mingled. Transfer them to a bowl.

4. Using a little more oil if necessary, place a tortilla in the pan. Place one portion of the vegetable mixture and a spoonful of cheese in the center of the tortilla.

5. Fold over the two sides and cook for a few moments to let the cheese melt. Remove, and keep the pancake warm in the oven while you make the rest.

6. Place the enchiladas on a warm serving plate and place a dollop of the guacamole mixture on each or use more cheese; decorate with the tomato slices ∎

PERU

Lima bean casserole

Serves 4

After its silver deposits were mined out, Peru's main export became guano (fertilizer from sea-bird droppings) until the late 19th century. Then saltpeter, used to preserve foods and make gunpowder, took over as the front-runner. Today the main exports are copper and zinc. Although nearly half the population works on the land, only three per cent of Peru's land area is given over to arable and permanent crops; main foods grown are rice, corn/maize, sorghum, potatoes and fruit.

INGREDIENTS

1¼ cups / 225 g Lima or butter beans, cooked

1 onion, chopped

2 cloves garlic, crushed

½ teaspoon chili powder

4 tomatoes, chopped

rind and juice of ½-1 lemon

2 tablespoons fresh parsley, chopped

oil

salt and pepper

1. Take a bowl and place the cooked beans in it; partially mash them with a potato masher or fork.

2. Now heat the oil and gently fry the onion for a minute or two. Then add the garlic and chili powder and cook for a few moments more.

3. The mashed beans can be spooned in at this point; mix them in well. Add the tomatoes, lemon rind and juice, parsley and seasoning. Cook, covered, for 5-10 minutes more to let the flavors fuse and then serve with pitta bread, tortilla chips or rice ■

ALGERIA

Thetchouka

Serves 4

Algeria's recent history has a strong connection with food, with wheat in particular. At the end of the 18th century, when Algeria was part of the Ottoman (Turkish) empire, the French revolutionary government bought large amounts of the wheat, but did not pay for it. Apparently the Bey (governor) of Algiers became so incensed at the French excuses that he slapped a French official. This gave the French the pretext to send in their soldiers and so achieve a long ambition: to set up a colony handily placed opposite their own shores.

Thetchouka is cousin to *chakchouka* in Morocco and to the French dish *pipérade* – all are dishes which combine tomatoes and bell peppers with eggs. In this one, beaten eggs are poured over the top of the cooked vegetables and baked until they set.

I N G R E D I E N T S

1 onion, chopped

3 cloves garlic, crushed

1 chili, sliced

2 bell peppers, sliced into thin strips lengthwise

6 tomatoes, chopped

4 eggs, beaten

oil

salt and pepper

Heat oven to 350°F/180°C/Gas 4

1. If you have one, use a pan that can transfer to the oven. Heat the oil and cook the onion for a few minutes before adding the garlic, chili and bell peppers.

2. When they have softened, put in the tomatoes and the seasoning. Let the mixture cook for 5 minutes, and stir from time to time.

3. Now pour the beaten eggs on top and bake in the oven for 10-15 minutes or until the eggs are set as you like them ■

EGYPT

Ful medames (Brown bean casserole)

Serves 4

Ful is the word for brown beans, but it can also be used specifically to mean this dish. It is best to cook the beans very slowly in a low oven as the recipe indicates, but if you want to reduce the cooking time, use a pressure cooker for seven minutes and then continue by the method below.

I N G R E D I E N T S

1 cup / 225 g field/ful brown beans, soaked

1 quart / 1 liter water

4 cloves garlic, crushed

1 tablespoon ground cumin

6 hard-boiled eggs, halved

1 teaspoon turmeric

2 tablespoons fresh parsley, chopped

4 tomatoes, sliced

2 lemons, cut into wedges

1 teaspoon paprika

6 tablespoons olive oil

salt

Heat oven to 300°F/150°C/Gas 2

1. Place the beans in an ovenproof casserole on top of the cooker with the water, garlic, 3 tablespoons of the oil and the cumin. Heat up and when the water is boiling, cover the pan and boil for 10 minutes.

2. Transfer the beans to the oven and let them cook very slowly for 3-4 hours (less if they are partially cooked already – see above) until they are soft. Season.

3. Put the hard-boiled eggs on a plate and dust them with the turmeric. Pour the olive oil into a jug or dish (or use the bottle); arrange the tomato slices, parsley and lemon wedges on dishes to be handed round separately.

4. Sprinkle the paprika on the ful before bringing the casserole to the table. Place the side dish ingredients around it so people can help themselves ■

Man selling oranges, Egypt.   Photo: Maximilien Bruggmann.

EGYPT

Labaneya (Yogurt and spinach soup)

Serves 6

Nearly all Egypt's people live in the fertile Nile valley and delta. The flooding of the Nile set a pattern for the country's economic life thousands of years ago. Nowadays the waters are controlled by dams like the Aswan which have enabled farmers to cultivate cash crops such as cotton and sugar in addition to their food crops – wheat, rice and vegetables such as potatoes and tomatoes.

Throughout history, especially in hot climates, milk has been used in its soured or fermented forms. Surplus milk could be preserved in this way as butter, cheese or – as in this recipe – yogurt.

INGREDIENTS

1 onion, sliced

2 pounds / 1 kg spinach, torn into strips

$^1/_2$ cup / 110 g rice

2 cups / 440 g yogurt

2-3 cloves garlic, crushed

3 tablespoons oil

1 quart / 1 liter warm water

salt and pepper

1. Using a large pan, heat the oil and then add the onion and cook until it is soft.

2. Now put in the spinach and combine it with the onion; cook them gently for about 10 minutes.

3. The rice goes in now. Stir it in to the onion and spinach mixture and then pour in the water, salt and pepper. Bring to the boil and let the rice simmer for 10-20 minutes until it is soft. Take the pan off the heat.

4. Turn the yogurt into a bowl and beat it with the crushed garlic. When that is done, spoon the yogurt mix into the soup and stir well. Then return the saucepan to the heat and cook very gently just to warm the soup. Take care not to let it boil as this will curdle the yogurt ■

MIDDLE EAST

Mahasha (Stuffed tomatoes)

Serves 4

Tomatoes originated in Central America and were taken to Europe in the 16th century by the Spanish. These fruits were probably orange-yellow in color, giving rise to one of their early names – 'golden apple' or *pomodoro*. Tomatoes are a popular ingredient of Mediterranean dishes and Egypt is one of the main producers.

For this recipe, instead of mashed potatoes for the filling you can use cooked rice or bulghur.

I N G R E D I E N T S

4 marmande or other large tomatoes

2 tablespoons fresh cilantro/coriander leaves, chopped

$^1/_2$ pound / 225 g potatoes, mashed

$^1/_3$ cup / 60 g peas

1 teaspoon curry powder

$^1/_2$-1 teaspoon chili powder

2 teaspoons cumin seeds

1 teaspoon mustard seeds

1 clove garlic, crushed

oil

salt

Heat oven to 325°F/160°C/Gas 3

1. To begin, slice the tomatoes in half and carefully scoop out the pulp and seeds; keep these for later use.

2. Then heat up some oil in a pan and when it is very hot, toss in the cilantro/coriander leaves and let them crisp up.

3. Now add the curry powder, chili, cumin seeds, mustard seeds and garlic to the fried cilantro/coriander leaves. Mix well and sprinkle on salt as required.

4. Cook for a minute or two before adding the mashed potato or bulghur, the peas and the tomato pulp. Stir all the ingredients well to distribute the spices.

5. Fill the tomatoes with the mixture and place them in a shallow ovenproof dish. Bake for 15-20 minutes and serve hot or cold ■

MOROCCO

Couscous

Serves 4-6

The classic North African dish uses *couscous* made of semolina. Semolina comes from 'hard' or durum wheat which, after milling, leaves small hard grains. *Couscous* is cooked by steaming over the sauce in a *couscousière* but you can get by with putting the *couscous* in a sieve, and sitting this above the cooking vegetables in a saucepan, with a lid on top. Apparently the name is onomatopoeic, from the rushing sound of the escaping steam.

I N G R E D I E N T S

¹/₂ cup / 85 g garbanzos/chickpeas, cooked (keep the water)

¹/₂ cup / 60 g white cabbage, finely sliced

1 onion, chopped

1 cup / 150 g turnip, chopped +

1 carrot, sliced

3 cloves

1 teaspoon cinnamon

¹/₂ teaspoon ground ginger

1 teaspoon paprika

2 zucchini/courgettes, sliced

1 egg-plant/aubergine, chopped

4 tomatoes, cut into quarters

¹/₂ cup / 50 g sultanas or raisins

2 tablespoons fresh cilantro/coriander leaves, chopped

¹/₄ teaspoon chili powder

¹/₄ cup / 50 ml tomato juice

¹/₂ pound / 225 g couscous

1 tablespoon margarine or oil

salt and pepper

+ optional ingredient

1. To begin, shake the couscous into a bowl and dampen it with a little warm water. Stir it and leave the grain to swell for about 15 minutes.

2. Now put the garbanzos/chickpeas and their water in a large pan and add the cabbage, onion, turnip and carrot together with the cloves, cinnamon, ginger and paprika. Bring to the boil and cook until the vegetables are almost tender.

3. The zucchini/courgettes, egg-plant/aubergine, tomatoes, sultanas or raisins, cilantro/coriander leaves, chili powder, tomato juice can all go in at this point, along with the salt and pepper.

4. Place the couscous into a sieve (with a lid over) or couscousière and steam it above the cooking vegetables for 20-30 minutes.

5. When everything is ready, spoon the couscous into a warmed serving dish and mix in a little margarine. Serve the vegetables separately ∎

cinnamon and cumin and cook for 2 minutes.

2. Now add the apples and sugar if using, and cook gently, turning so that the fruit is coated in the spices.

3. When the apple pieces are soft, put in the beans and just enough of their cooking water to cover the bottom of the pan.

4. Season and stir before simmering for 5-10 minutes to let the flavors combine. Serve with a bowl of yogurt and boiled rice or cracked wheat ■

SAUDI ARABIA

Apple beanpot

Serves 4

'Comfort me with apples for I am sick,' said King Solomon, thus perhaps sparking the notion that an apple a day keeps the doctor away. However, some believe that the apples King Solomon referred to were in fact apricots. It seems that these were abundant in Palestine at the time, whereas apples were not.

I N G R E D I E N T S

$^1/_2$ onion, sliced

$^1/_2$ teaspoon turmeric

$^1/_2$ teaspoon ground allspice

$^1/_2$ teaspoon cinnamon

$^1/_2$ teaspoon cumin

2 cooking apples, chopped into small cubes

$1^1/_4$ cups / 225 g Lima or butter beans, cooked (retain the water)

1 teaspoon sugar +

2 cups / 440 g yogurt

2 tablespoons margarine or oil

salt and pepper

+ optional ingredient

1. First heat the margarine or oil and sauté the onion until it is golden. At this point, sprinkle in the turmeric, allspice,

SYRIA

Imam bayaldi (Stuffed egg-plant/aubergine)

Serves 4

'The Imam (priest) swooned' is the translation of this dish, and the usual explanations are either that he fainted with delight when he tasted it, or that he swooned at the thought of how expensive it must have been to make. I don't think either of these sound plausible: it tastes pleasant but is not the kind of thing to knock you out. And egg-plant/aubergine was unlikely to have been that expensive in a part of the world where they are readily available. Maybe he had been in a rush and been running, and all the excitement was too much for him.

I N G R E D I E N T S

4 egg-plants/aubergines

1 onion, finely sliced

4 cloves garlic, crushed

1 green bell pepper, chopped

6 tomatoes, chopped

squeeze of lemon juice

1 tablespoon fresh parsley, chopped

**1 cup / 100 g monterrey jack or cheddar cheese, grated
  or 1 cup / 225 g yogurt**

oil

salt and pepper

Heat oven to 325°F/160°C/Gas 3

1. First of all, put the egg-plants/aubergines into the oven to cook for 10 minutes or so.

2. While they are baking, heat the oil in a pan and cook the onion until it turns soft and transparent. Now add the garlic and stir this round for a few moments but do not let it brown.

3. The green bell pepper goes in next, and when it has softened put in the tomatoes. Continue to cook gently for a few minutes.

4. Meanwhile, remove the egg-plants/aubergines from the oven and when they are cool enough to handle, cut off the stalk end and slice them in halves, lengthwise.

5. Remove as much of the pulp as you can, using a teaspoon or sharp knife, without damaging the skins. Chop up the pulp and add it to the pan with the onion and other vegetables. Squeeze in some lemon juice and season.

6. Arrange the egg-plant/aubergine halves in an ovenproof dish and pile the cooked mixture into them, and around them if there is some left over.

7. Put the dish into the oven for 10 minutes, with the cheese on top if using, and cook for a few minutes or until the cheese has melted and turned golden.

8. Remove from the oven, scatter the parsley over and serve either hot or cold, with yogurt if using ■

> **IN ALL RECIPES**
> ● **PEPPER AND SALT ARE TO TASTE.**
> ● **CHILI AND SUGAR ARE GIVEN AS GUIDE QUANTITIES ONLY.**
> **VARY TO TASTE.**
> ● **MEASURES FOR BEANS AND GRAINS REFER TO DRY INGREDIENTS.**

TUNISIA

Broad bean tajine/eggeh (Omelette)

Serves 4

Tunisia, Algeria, Morocco and Libya are the North African states which form the *Maghreb* – the western Islamic world, as distinct from the *Mashreq* or eastern Islamic countries.

The *tajine* is a favorite dish in North Africa, and it crops up – as *tajen*, *tagine*, *tadjin* or *tagin* – over much of the Middle East. *Tajine* is usually cooked in an earthenware pot (also named *tajine*) over a charcoal fire, although in Tunisia the same name is used for the omelette-like *eggeh*. This is picnic fare in the Middle East, the equivalent of sandwiches or pizza.

There are many variations and you could use cooked black-eyed beans with two sliced bell peppers and a couple of tomatoes, or French beans, instead of fresh broad beans for this recipe.

INGREDIENTS

2 cups / 225 g broad beans (canned or frozen will do)

6 eggs

4 scallions/spring onions, finely sliced

juice of $^1/_2$ lemon

1 tablespoon margarine or oil

salt and pepper

1. Begin by boiling the beans for a few minutes until they are tender; drain.

2. Then beat the eggs and mix them with the beans, scallions/spring onions, lemon juice, salt and pepper.

3. Heat the oil or margarine in a pan and when it is sizzling pour in the egg and bean mixture. Put a cover on the pan and cook for 15-20 minutes over a gentle heat.

4. To brown the top, place the pan under the grill for a few minutes. The omelette can be served hot or cold, cut into wedges ■

SIDE DISHES

Women at the vegetable market, Guerrero, Mexico. Photo: Liba Taylor/Hutchison Photo Library.

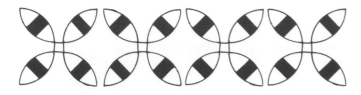

1 tablespoon red wine vinegar

$^1/_2$ cup / 120 ml water

$^1/_2$ cup / 50 g paprika

2 tablespoons chili powder

2 teaspoons salt

$^1/_2$ teaspoon ground black pepper

$^1/_4$ teaspoon fresh ginger, grated

seeds from 1 cardamom pod, crushed

$^1/_4$ teaspoon ground coriander

$^1/_4$ teaspoon ground fenugreek seeds

$^1/_4$ teaspoon ground nutmeg

2 cloves, crushed

pinch cinnamon

pinch allspice

1. Combine the garlic, onion, vinegar and water in a blender until smooth. Set aside.

2. Now put all the remaining ingredients in a heavy pan and cook them, dry, over a medium heat stirring constantly until they are toasted. Then let them cool a while.

3. At this point, transfer the garlic and onion mixture from the blender to the pan with the spices and stir it in. Then heat up the pan again and cook over a low heat, stirring often, for 10 minutes until the berberé reduces to the consistency of a thick paste.

4. Allow to cool and then spoon it into a jar and keep in the refrigerator, covered. It will keep for a month or so ■

ETHIOPIA

Berberé paste

Makes about $^1/_2$ cup (enough for two or so *wats* (stews), see pps.62 and 63)

In Amharic, Ethiopia's official language, *berberé* means pure red chili powder but it is also used for a red pepper-spice paste that is an essential ingredient of Ethiopian cuisine. The paste gives fire to the *wat* (stew), the national dish of the country, which can be made of meat or vegetables.

Use 2-3 teaspoons of the paste to 4 servings of stew, or more if you like a stronger taste.

I N G R E D I E N T S

1 clove garlic, crushed

1 scallion/spring onion, white part only or 1 teaspoon sliced onion

KENYA

Kachumbari (Chili relish)

Serves 4

'*Kachumbari* was originally a coastal speciality but it is now widespread in Kenya, especially in urban areas. This relish or sambal spices up a range of dishes from snacks such as *kosie* (p.36) to main dishes like *irio* (p.69) or *soy beans and palaver* (p.66). It needs to stand for a good 4 hours before you use it, and will keep in the refrigerator for a week or so.' *Phoebe Omondi, Nairobi, Kenya*

I N G R E D I E N T S

1/2 chili, finely chopped

4 tomatoes, chopped

2 handfuls parsley, chopped

2 cloves of garlic, crushed

1 red bell pepper, sliced

1/2 onion, very finely chopped or grated

1 lemon or lime

1 tablespoon water

salt and pepper

1. Put the chili, tomatoes and parsley into a serving bowl which has a lid.

2. In a separate bowl, blender or mortar, mash or pound the crushed garlic together with the bell pepper and onion. When well mixed, add to the serving bowl containing the other ingredients.

3. The lemon or lime juice can be squeezed in now, before adding one tablespoon of water. Combine all the ingredients well – the mixture can be put in the blender if you wish. Cover and leave to stand for at least 4 hours before serving as a pickle or relish ■

MALAWI

Boiled pumpkin

Serves 4

Malawi's boundaries, like those of many African countries, were a colonial invention. With its lake and green hills the country reminded Scottish missionaries and settlers of their highland glens – a connection given substance in town names like Blantyre. It is one of the most densely settled areas of Central Africa, with relatively few cattle and a wide range of food crops including millet, corn/maize, beans, lentils and garbanzos/chickpeas. Hastings Kamuzu Banda has been President since 1964 and President for Life since 1971.

'Pumpkin makes a common accompaniment to stews in this part of Africa, its sweetness balancing the savory ingredients.' *Monica Macmillan, Lusaka, Zambia*

I N G R E D I E N T S

1/2 onion, sliced

2 scallions/spring onions, sliced +

1 pound / 450 g pumpkin, chopped

1 tablespoon parsley, chopped

a little water

1/2 teaspoon sugar +

2 tablespoons oil

salt and pepper

+ optional ingredients

1. Heat the oil and sauté the onion followed by the scallions/ spring onions if using.

2. When they are nicely softened, put in the pumpkin pieces and a little water barely to cover the base of the pan. Boil gently, with the lid on, for 10 minutes.

3. Then remove the cover and cook very slowly, stirring frequently so that the pumpkin does not catch, for 20 minutes or so, until it is cooked.

4. Season with salt and pepper and add a little sugar if liked. The dish can also be cooked in a low oven, uncovered for half an hour, after the initial 10-minute boiling period ■

MALAWI

Thelele (Okra/ladies' fingers)

Serves 2

'From the garden, pluck the fresh green okra fruits and store them in the shade, ready for making this dish.' *Thengo Chirombo, Blantyre, Malawi*

Okra, part of the mallow family, are one of Africa's indigenous vegetables. They are related to the cotton plant, and also to garden flowers such as the hollyhock and hibiscus. If you do not have okra in your garden (they need a tropical climate) you can buy them from a specialist vegetable store.

I N G R E D I E N T S

$^1/_2$ onion, chopped

$^1/_2$ pound / 225 g okra, topped and tailed, chopped into 2 or 3 pieces

1 teaspoon garam masala

4 tomatoes, chopped

$^1/_2$ pound / 225 g spinach or pumpkin leaves, chopped

a little water

oil

salt and pepper

1. Begin by heating the oil and then gently cook the onion for 2 minutes. Add the okra pieces and sauté them with the onion until they are slightly browned.

2. At this point, sprinkle on the garam masala and fry for a further minute before adding the tomatoes.

3. Let these ingredients simmer together for 5 minutes or so, stirring from time to time, and then toss in the chopped pumpkin leaves or spinach.

4. Now pour in just enough water to cover the base of the pan. Put the lid on, and simmer for 10 minutes.

5. After this, stir the vegetables and season. If the mixture looks too liquid, remove the cover and continue to simmer, letting some of the water boil off before you serve ■

NIGERIA

Funkaso (Millet pancakes)

Makes 10-15

With an estimated 108 million people, Nigeria is Africa's most populous country. Oil dominates the economy, with cocoa, rubber and timber as the main agricultural exports. Most of the farming is done on small-holdings growing crops like sorghum, corn/maize, cassava/manioc, yams, millet and rice. Plantations are gaining ground producing raw materials for corporate use – such as grain for breweries. Nigerians are great beer drinkers. There are over 30 local brands including *Star*, *Gold*, and *Double Crown*.

The batter for these pancakes needs to stand for about 4 hours before you start cooking. It helps if you have a flat pancake griddle, but if you do not then use a heavy fry-pan and a good bendy utensil to turn and lift the *funkaso*. They are similar to (though smaller than) the Ethiopian *injera* which are made from a millet-relative called *teff,* and they can be served with Ethiopian dishes such as the *wats* on pps. 62 and 63.

I N G R E D I E N T S

2 cups / 250 g millet flour

1¼ cups/ 300 ml lukewarm water

margarine or oil

sugar to taste

pinch of salt

1. Sift the flour into a bowl and gradually pour in the warm water, stirring and mixing well as you do so to make a smooth, runny paste. Set aside for 4 hours.

2. After this, heat the margarine or oil in a shallow pan or griddle plate. While it is warming, beat the batter with a spoon.

3. When the margarine or oil is hot, ladle or pour enough batter into the pan to make a saucer-sized pancake and cook until crisp. You can turn it once if you like but it is not essential. Remove and keep warm.

4. Cook the others in the same way and serve to accompany a main dish, or as a snack with honey, or chutney ■

SIERRA LEONE

Frejon (Beans with cocoa)

Serves 4

'I've heard that cocoa is an important food for the British and French,' says Ghanaian cocoa farmer, Kwabena Nten. 'They say that the whites dote on sugary things and they make "chocolate" with it. What do I need chocolate for? My stomach knows only plantain and cocoyam.'

Cocoa was introduced to West Africa from Latin America and is a major export crop for countries such as Ghana, Sierra Leone and Côte d'Ivoire. Although there is some local processing, you won't find much chocolate in the region.

The *frejons* of Nigeria and West Africa are purées made of

beans flavored with cocoa and enhanced by coconut milk and eaten particularly by Christians on Good Friday. Then sugar is added and the dish is eaten as a pudding. But it makes a pleasant accompanying dish to savory dishes as well.

I N G R E D I E N T S

1 cup / 225 g cowpeas/black-eyed beans, cooked

½ cup / 120 ml coconut milk

1 teaspoon ground mixed spice

1-2 tablespoons cocoa powder, mixed to a paste with a little water

1-2 tablespoons sugar

pinch of salt

1. Drain the cooked beans and put them into a bowl containing the coconut milk and sugar. Mix well and then partially mash them with a fork.

2. Now add the cocoa paste, the mixed spice and a pinch of salt; stir them in. Return all the ingredients to a saucepan and heat gently so that the flavors mingle before serving ■

Tomato vendor, Lilongwe market, Malawi. *Photo: Rob Whitrow/Robert Harding.*

SOUTH AFRICA

Glazed sweet potatoes

Serves 4

Sweet potatoes were a Portuguese introduction to Africa from Latin America. Their Xhosa name, *batata*, is the same as the Portuguese word, as in the famous Portuguese phrase *'vá plantar batatas!'* (Go and plant potatoes – get lost!). They are grown and eaten widely throughout southern Africa and have been a staple for black peasants and small-holders, as well as for the settlers. Nowadays sweet potatoes are being edged out by 'Irish' or round potatoes – as in fish and chips and other oily potato concoctions.

This is a typical Cape recipe with its use of cinnamon and sweet and sour tastes.

I N G R E D I E N T S

1 teaspoon sugar or honey

1 tablespoon raisins or sultanas

$^{1}/_{2}$ teaspoon ground ginger

1 teaspoon cinnamon

juice of a lemon

grated rind of an orange

2 sweet potatoes, sliced and parboiled

a little water

2 tablespoons margarine

salt

1. Melt the margarine in a heavy pan and mix in the sugar or honey as well as the raisins or sultanas.

2. Next add the ginger, cinnamon, salt, lemon juice and orange rind. Mix well before pouring in a little water. Now put in the partially-cooked potato slices and stir them round to coat them in the sauce.

3. Cover the pan and let the potatoes cook very gently for 5-10 minutes, turning them from time to time so that they cook evenly and do not catch ■

UGANDA

Green vegetables with coconut milk

Serves 4

In the film *Mississippi Masala* we get a glimpse of Idi Amin's Uganda and the expulsion of the Asian community. This beautiful country has suffered war and disruption ever since, and is trying to climb out of its dire economic and social position. Uganda is almost totally dependent on coffee exports for foreign exchange. But President Museveni's integrity and commitment to democracy have kept hopes of improvement alive for ordinary people.

I N G R E D I E N T S

1 onion, chopped

2 pounds / 1 kg spinach, kale or other green vegetables, chopped

1 cup / 240 ml coconut milk

a few slices of red bell pepper

salt

1. Pour in just enough water to cover the base of a large saucepan and bring it to the boil. Then put in the onion and let it cook for a few minutes before adding the green vegetables. Steam-simmer, covered, for 5 minutes.

2. After this pour in the coconut milk; season, and stir well to integrate the ingredients.

3. Let the mixture cook for another 20 minutes, with the cover off, and then serve hot, garnished with the red bell pepper slices, with rice or corn/maize meal porridge, nshima (see p.112) ■

ZAMBIA

Nshima (Corn/maize meal porridge) **with spinach sauce**

Serves 4-6

Corn/maize meal is commonly called 'mielie meal' in southern Africa, from the Portuguese word for maize, *milho*. Since its introduction to Africa from South America about 200 years ago, corn/maize has become a mainstay food but its need for water can make it a liability in drought periods. The crops it has supplanted, millet and sorghum, can survive on less water.

'*Nshima* is Zambia's staple dish, often served with a spinach or greens relish like the one below. Most relishes are quite substantial, more like a sauce or stew.' *Mary Namakando, Lusaka, Zambia*

I N G R E D I E N T S

2 cups / 300 g corn/maize meal

water

1. Put the meal into a large pan and just cover with water, stirring carefully. Bring the mixture to the boil and then let it simmer for about 5 minutes to make a porridge.

2. When the mixture begins to come away from the sides of the pan, remove from the heat and serve at once, with a relish such as the one below. People tear off small chunks of the nshima and use them to scoop up relishes, stews and soups.

RAPE OR SPINACH RELISH OR SAUCE

1 onion, sliced

2 tomatoes, chopped

2 pounds / 1 kg rape or spinach, finely chopped

2-3 tablespoons oil

salt

1. Heat the oil in a large pan and then sauté the onion for 2 minutes. Add the tomatoes now and cook for 1-2 minutes.

2. Turn up the heat and put in the spinach; cook it quickly in the hot oil.

3. Season, and mix well before serving hot with the freshly-made nshima ∎

Tomato and peanut relish or sauce

Serves 4

Peanuts, known as groundnuts in Africa, are protein-rich and excellent for vegetarian dishes. Despite their name, they are really beans or legumes. They grew originally in South America but are now widely cultivated as a food and also as a cash crop in West Africa. Peanuts have more or less displaced the African equivalent, the Bambara groundnut.

'This tomato and groundnut (peanut) relish is found in Zambia and Malawi and often has beans and other vegetables added to it. Peanuts/groundnuts are commonly put into relishes when no meat is available.' *Irene Wilkie, Edinburgh, UK*

I N G R E D I E N T S

1 onion, sliced

$1/2$ pound / 225 g tomatoes, chopped

1 cup / 125 g peanuts, ground

$1/2$ teaspoon chili powder

1 tablespoon soy sauce

1 tablespoon oil

salt

1. First heat the oil and then sauté the onion until it is soft.

2. Now put in the tomatoes and cook them until they begin to break down.

3. At this point, add the ground peanuts and stir until everything blends well. Sprinkle on the chili powder, pour in the soy sauce, and season.

4. Continue to cook, adding some water if necessary to make the consistency you prefer, and then serve with nshima (p.112) or rice ∎

ZANZIBAR

Mkate wa ufute (Pancakes)

Makes 8-10

Zanzibar's name comes from the Arab word 'Zandj': 'Zandjibar' meaning 'the coast of the Blacks'. After the Portuguese were driven out of the area by the Sultan of Oman, Zanzibar became the Sultan's place of residence. Between 1698 and 1830, Zanzibar and the coast (now Tanzania) remained under the rule of the Oman Sultanate.

'This bread is made by Zanzibari Arabs, and it can be eaten with main meals or served as a snack with jam, or chutney.'
Rosemary Budd, Leicester, UK

I N G R E D I E N T S

1 teaspoon dried yeast

1 teaspoon sugar

2/3 cup / 150 ml warm water

1 cup / 125 g flour

2/3 cup / 150 ml milk

3 tablespoons sesame seeds, toasted

oil

1. Put the yeast and sugar into a bowl and pour on the warm water. Let it activate for 5-10 minutes until it becomes frothy.

2. Shake or sift the flour into a large bowl. Make a well in the center and pour in the yeast mixture, stirring as you do so.

3. After that, gradually add the milk, stirring continuously to make a thick batter.

4. Now heat a little oil in a frying pan. When it is very hot, spoon in some of the batter and spread it out into a circle, using the back of the spoon.

5. Let the pancake cook for 2 minutes on one side before turning over to brown the second side.

6. Sprinkle on the toasted sesame seeds for the final few minutes of cooking; then remove and keep hot while you cook the rest ∎

AFGHANISTAN

Egg-plant/aubergine in yogurt

Serves 4

After the years of war, about six million Afghani refugees live abroad – mainly in Pakistan and Iran. Over 65 per cent of the labor force used to work on the land, but the war greatly disrupted food production. It is reckoned that out of 22,000 farming villages, more than 12,000 have been abandoned or destroyed. The main food crops are wheat, fruit and vegetables, and livestock-rearing is also important.

I N G R E D I E N T S

2 egg-plants/aubergines, diced
1 teaspoon ground coriander
1 teaspoon ground cumin
$^1/_2$ teaspoon ground cinnamon
$^1/_2$ onion, sliced finely
$^3/_4$ cup / 150 g yogurt
$^1/_4$ teaspoon chili powder
$^1/_2$ teaspoon garam masala
oil
salt

1. To begin, place the egg-plant/aubergine pieces in a bowl or colander, sprinkle on some salt to draw out the bitter taste, and leave them for 20 minutes. Then rinse and drain.

2. Heat the oil in a wok or pan and sizzle the coriander, cumin and cinnamon for 30 seconds before adding the onion.

3. Stir-fry that for a few minutes and then put in about half of the egg-plant/aubergine pieces.

4. When these begin to soften, remove them and stir-fry the rest, adding more oil as necessary.

5. The first batch of vegetables and spices can be replaced now; stir all the ingredients together. Cook until the egg plant/aubergines are soft (about 5 minutes in a wok, up to 20 minutes in a saucepan).

6. When they are ready, turn down the heat and spoon in the yogurt, stirring well. Simmer very gently – not too hot or the yogurt will curdle – for 15 minutes and then serve, garnished with the chili powder and garam masala sprinkled on top ∎

BANGLADESH

Brindaboni (Snowpeas/mangetout and sweet potatoes)

Serves 4-6

'The name of this dish is derived from the Brindabon forests of North India where the tales of Radha and Krishna were supposed to have been enacted. There is a distinctly Vaishnav (from Vishnu, a Hindu god) influence in this dish, shown by the omission of onions, and the special combination of spices which blends very well with the vegetables.' *Meghna Guhathakurta, Dhaka, Bangladesh*

I N G R E D I E N T S

1 teaspoon cumin seeds
1 teaspoon coriander seeds
1 teaspoon turmeric
2 bayleaves
2 sweet potatoes, thinly sliced
$^1/_2$ pound / 225 g snowpeas/mangetout,
  cut into 2 or 3 sections
oil
salt

1. First of all, toast the cumin and coriander seeds by heating them in a frying pan, without oil, shaking from time to time or moving them with a wooden spoon until they go a little brown. Then crush them in a mortar and set aside.

Saag (Spinach)

Serves 4

'The rivers which criss-cross Bangladesh supply its people with one of their main foods, fish; while many vitamins come from the range of vegetables grown in the fertile soil of the country's kitchen gardens. Spinach or *palong saag* is one of these vegetables which is sold in the market in the winter season and is a popular starter or side dish.' *Meghna Guhathakurta, Dhaka, Bangladesh*

I N G R E D I E N T S

1 clove garlic, crushed

1 dried red chili *

1 pound / 450 g spinach, chopped

1 green chili, chopped

oil

salt

* If the chili is not broken or chopped, and therefore the seeds are not released, then the chili will not make the dish hot but will impart a smoky flavor. Discard the chili before serving if desired.

If you do not want a chili to be too hot, then cut it longitudinally and take out its seeds. The green or red skin provides vitamin C and also gives the dish a pungent taste.

1. Heat the oil and then toss in the crushed garlic and the whole dried red chili and let them sizzle for a few minutes.

2. Now add the spinach and stir-fry for 3 minutes. After this, put the lid on and let the spinach cook in its own steam; do not add water.

3. Cook for 10 minutes and then add the green chili slices and seasoning. Serve with lemon wedges or mustard ■

2. Now heat the oil in a heavy pan and add the turmeric, bayleaves and salt. Then put in the sweet potatoes and cook for 5 minutes, turning them frequently, until they begin to soften.

3. Add the cumin and coriander. Mix well.

4. Next pour in just enough water to cover the base of the pan and simmer, covered, for about 10 minutes or until the sweet potatoes are soft.

5. When they are almost ready, turn up the heat and put in the snowpeas/mangetout. Cook for 1-2 minutes and then serve ■

CORN OR MAIZE

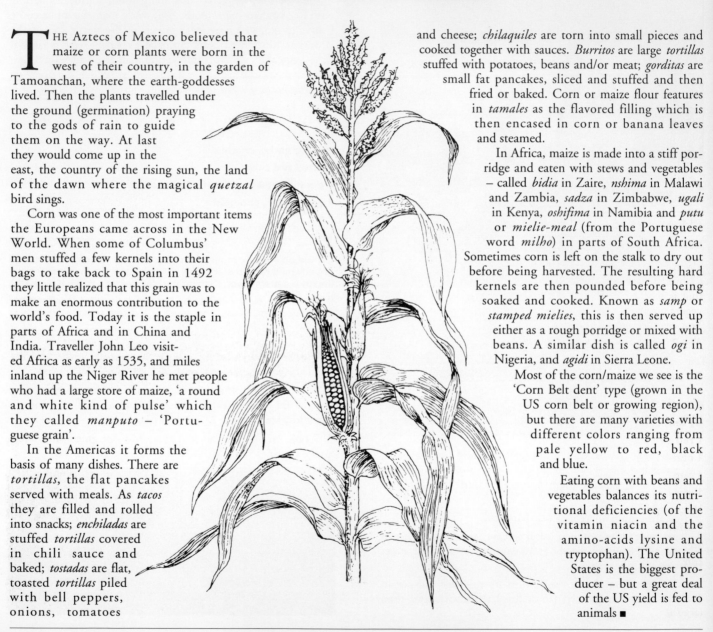

THE Aztecs of Mexico believed that maize or corn plants were born in the west of their country, in the garden of Tamoanchan, where the earth-goddesses lived. Then the plants travelled under the ground (germination) praying to the gods of rain to guide them on the way. At last they would come up in the east, the country of the rising sun, the land of the dawn where the magical *quetzal* bird sings.

Corn was one of the most important items the Europeans came across in the New World. When some of Columbus' men stuffed a few kernels into their bags to take back to Spain in 1492 they little realized that this grain was to make an enormous contribution to the world's food. Today it is the staple in parts of Africa and in China and India. Traveller John Leo visited Africa as early as 1535, and miles inland up the Niger River he met people who had a large store of maize, 'a round and white kind of pulse' which they called *manputo* – 'Portuguese grain'.

In the Americas it forms the basis of many dishes. There are *tortillas*, the flat pancakes served with meals. As *tacos* they are filled and rolled into snacks; *enchiladas* are stuffed *tortillas* covered in chili sauce and baked; *tostadas* are flat, toasted *tortillas* piled with bell peppers, onions, tomatoes and cheese; *chilaquiles* are torn into small pieces and cooked together with sauces. *Burritos* are large *tortillas* stuffed with potatoes, beans and/or meat; *gorditas* are small fat pancakes, sliced and stuffed and then fried or baked. Corn or maize flour features in *tamales* as the flavored filling which is then encased in corn or banana leaves and steamed.

In Africa, maize is made into a stiff porridge and eaten with stews and vegetables – called *bidia* in Zaire, *nshima* in Malawi and Zambia, *sadza* in Zimbabwe, *ugali* in Kenya, *oshifima* in Namibia and *putu* or *mielie-meal* (from the Portuguese word *milho*) in parts of South Africa. Sometimes corn is left on the stalk to dry out before being harvested. The resulting hard kernels are then pounded before being soaked and cooked. Known as *samp* or *stamped mielies*, this is then served up either as a rough porridge or mixed with beans. A similar dish is called *ogi* in Nigeria, and *agidi* in Sierra Leone.

Most of the corn/maize we see is the 'Corn Belt dent' type (grown in the US corn belt or growing region), but there are many varieties with different colors ranging from pale yellow to red, black and blue.

Eating corn with beans and vegetables balances its nutritional deficiencies (of the vitamin niacin and the amino-acids lysine and tryptophan). The United States is the biggest producer – but a great deal of the US yield is fed to animals ■

onions and ginger first and cook them for 1 minute, stirring all the time.

2. The bell pepper, carrot, snowpeas/mangetout and celery go in next. Stir-fry briskly for 2 minutes.

3. Now pour in the water and flavor with a few drops of soy sauce. Toss the vegetables around in the wok or pan so that they are all coated with soy and then increase the heat if necessary to bring the water to boiling point.

4. Cover the wok or pan, reduce the heat slightly, and cook for 2-3 minutes until the vegetables are crisp but tender. Serve at once ■

CHINA

Chinese vegetables

Serves 4-6

Even if you do not have the dexterity (or the cleaver) of a Chinese cook you can still make a delightful vegetable stir-fry that is colorful, fresh and delicious. It's best made with fresh vegetables, of course, but frozen or canned ones would do. You can use zucchini/courgettes, green beans and broccoli as well or instead of those listed below.

I N G R E D I E N T S

4 scallions/spring onions, sliced

$^1/_2$ teaspoon fresh ginger, grated

1 red bell pepper, sliced

1 carrot, thinly sliced

1 cup / 110 g snowpeas/mangetout

1 stalk celery, cut into thin diagonal slices

$^1/_3$ cup / 80 ml water

1 tablespoon soy sauce

oil

salt

1. After the vegetables are prepared, heat the oil in a wok or large frying pan. When it is hot, put in the scallions/spring

CHINA/HONG KONG

Fried noodles

Serves 4

After rice and steamed bread or dumplings, noodles are the main staple at Chinese tables. They come in many thicknesses and are made from a dough of buckwheat, wheat, rice or bean starch, mixed with differing amounts of egg and water. They are prepared in four ways: with bean-paste sauce; served in gravy; in soup; and fried as here.

These make a crispy accompaniment to main meals and salads. Try them also with non-Chinese meals.

I N G R E D I E N T S

EGG NOODLES

1/2 pound / 225 g Chinese thin egg noodles

water

oil

1. Cook the noodles in boiling water according to the directions on the package. Then drain in a colander.

2. Take a flat rectangular baking sheet or cookie tray and arrange 2 or 3 layers of kitchen paper on it. Then spread the noodles evenly on top and leave them to dry for 2-3 hours.

3. When that is done, heat about 2 inches/5 cms oil in a wok. Using a slotted spoon or tongs, cook a small batch of noodles at a time for about 30 seconds or until they are golden.

4. Then remove them and drain on absorbsent paper while you quickly cook the rest in the same way.

CHINESE VERMICELLI/BEAN THREADS

1/2 pound / 225 g vermicelli/bean threads

oil

1. First, cut the bundle of bean threads into two and then gently pull each half apart to make small bunches.

2. Heat enough oil in the wok to deep-fry (about 2 inches/ 5 cms) and when it is ready put in the bean threads, using a slotted spoon or tongs.

3. Cook for about 5 seconds until the vermicelli rises to the top. Then remove at once and drain on kitchen paper while you cook the rest in the same way ∎

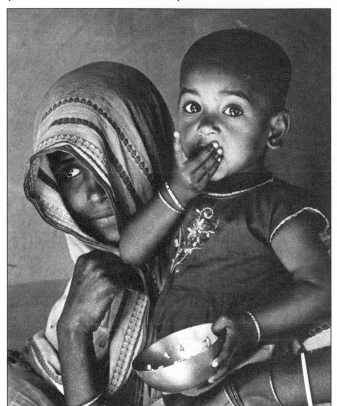

INDIA

Aloo bhaji (South Indian potatoes)

Serves 4

'This is a version of a very basic potato recipe, often found in *thali* dishes of affordable eating houses. The dish is usually served with *puris*, the deep-fried, fluffy wholewheat breads that are eaten in almost every part of India.' *Dinyar Godrej, Oxford, UK*

Asafoetida or *heeng*, used in this recipe, is a reddish dried gum resin with a strong smell and a garlicky flavor. Although dismissed as a 'culinary absurdity' by South African food writer Louis Leipoldt, *asafoetida* not only adds flavor but also aids digestion.

INGREDIENTS

1/4 teaspoon powdered asafoetida *

1/4 cup / 55 g urad dal†, soaked for 15 minutes

2 onions, sliced

1 pound / 450 g potatoes, cut into pieces and parboiled

1/2 teaspoon turmeric

3-4 tablespoons lemon juice

handful fresh cilantro/coriander leaves, chopped

2 tablespoons oil

salt

* Available from Asian stores. Omit if you cannot find it.

† Urad dal are the skinned, halved white insides of urad (small black beans), available in Asian stores.

1. Heat the oil in a saucepan and fry the asafoetida for 10-15 seconds. Then add the onions and sauté them for a minute.

2. Put in the drained dal now and fry it with the onions for a minute or so. At the end of this time, spoon in the potatoes, sprinkle on the turmeric and salt and stir well to mix them together.

3. Cook for 5-10 minutes until the onions, potatoes and dal are soft. Then stir in the lemon juice, scatter the cilantro/coriander leaves over and serve ■

Sour dal

Serves 4

For this recipe, you can use the hulled, split version of the African pigeon peas, known as *toor dal*. They are sold either as ordinary toor dal, or as 'oily' toor dal, because they are coated with an oil before packing. The oily version needs to be rinsed several times in hot water, then in cold, before use. You can use either type for this dish.

INGREDIENTS

1 cup / 225 g toor dal

1/2 teaspoon turmeric

2 1/2 cups / 590 ml water

1 teaspoon tamarind* soaked in 2 tablespoons warm water, or 2 tablespoons lemon juice

3 whole cloves

1/2 teaspoon cumin seeds

1/2 teaspoon fresh ginger, grated

1 teaspoon brown sugar +

margarine or ghee

salt and pepper

+ optional ingredient

* Tamarind is usually obtainable, in block form, in Asian grocery stores. Simply cut off what you need and store the rest in the refrigerator.

1. Place the dal in a saucepan with the turmeric and water and bring to the boil. Then reduce the heat and cook slowly for about 30 minutes until the dal is soft and the water absorbed.

2. When the tamarind has soaked for 10 minutes, press it with a fork or spoon while still soaking to extract its juice. Then place it in a sieve over the bowl and rub with a spoon to force through the brown pulp. Pour the tamarind water, or lemon juice if using this instead, into the dal and add the seasoning.

3. Now heat the margarine or ghee in a separate pan and cook the cloves together with the cumin seeds and ginger for a few minutes.

4. Add these ingredients to the dal now and sprinkle in some sugar if using.

5. Let the dal cook very gently, or re-heat the next day. It should be quite dry but add more liquid if you wish ■

Woman cooking chapatis, Rajastan, India. *Photo: Maximilien Bruggmann.*

Phulkas and chapatis (Flat breads)

Makes approximately 12 phulkas

Phulkas are small and thin and they should puff up in the last stages of cooking. *Chapatis* are made from the same dough but are larger and thicker. A correspondent recalled an episode in Agra when he saw an elephant and his *mahout* (rider) stop outside an apartment building. Shouting up to his wife, the *mahout* received a newspaper-wrapped parcel let down on string from an upstairs window. Opening the package, he gave *chapatis*, six at a time, to his elephant. The animal was obviously used to this, curving back its trunk regularly to receive the snack.

I N G R E D I E N T S

2 cups / 250 g flour

1/2 cup / 120 ml water

salt

1. Put the flour and salt into a bowl. Make a well in the middle and pour in half the water. Mix well with your hands to make a dough. If the mixture seems too dry, add more water. Shape the dough into a ball.

2. Turn the dough onto a floured board and knead it for 10-15 minutes until it becomes smooth and elastic. Then cover it with a damp cloth and set it aside for 30 minutes.

3. After this time, knead the dough again for 5 minutes. Divide it into walnut-sized pieces. Shape each piece into a ball and roll them out into rounds measuring about 5 inches/10 cms across.

4. Now lightly grease a heavy fry pan or griddle and heat it. When it is hot, place one of the dough circles on it and cook, rotating it with your fingers or a spoon, for 1-2 minutes or until bubbles appear on the top. Then flip it over and cook the other side in the same way.

5. If you have a gas cooker, grip the phulka using a metal utensil (barbecue tongs, or even nutcrackers) and hold it vertically over the flame until it puffs up. If you are using an electric stove, leave the phulka on the griddle and, using kitchen paper or a cloth, press it down firmly from all sides for a few moments. It will puff up when the pressure is released ■

INDONESIA

Nasi minyak (Fragrant rice)

Serves 4

Indonesia has a special place in the history of food as its spices, such as cinnamon and cloves, were the spur to much early trade. Cinnamon was known in Egypt as early as 1450 BC. In Indonesia today, the bulk of the clove harvest is used in the distinctive local cigarettes, *kretek*. Five-spice powder or 'five-fragrance powder' – made from anise seed, star anise, cloves, cinnamon and peppercorns – can be found in Chinese stores.

I N G R E D I E N T S

1 onion, sliced finely

2 cloves garlic, crushed

1 teaspoon turmeric

1/2 teaspoon five-spice powder *

2 tablespoons almond flakes

1 cup / 225 g rice

2 tablespoons ghee, margarine or oil

1 1/2 cups / 350 ml water

salt

* Obtainable from Chinese stores. If you cannot obtain this, then use the same quantity of ground mixed spice.

1. Heat the oil in a large saucepan and then sauté the onion and garlic for a few minutes until they soften.

2. Now put in the turmeric, spice powder, 1 tablespoon of the almond flakes and salt and cook for a little longer.

3. Add the rice and fry it for 2-3 minutes, stirring all the time. When you have done this, pour in the water and bring the pan to the boil, giving the rice an occasional stir.

4. Once it is boiling, cover the pot and turn down the heat as low as possible while maintaining a simmering heat. Cook the rice until all the liquid has been absorbed and the grains are fluffy. If necessary, add more water.

5. Just before serving, scatter the remaining almond flakes over the top ■

SOUTH EAST ASIA

Chutneys, relishes and sambals

Mint and cilantro/coriander chutney

This chutney goes well with just about any Indian meal and makes an especially good dip to go with *phulkas/chapatis* (p. 121), *samosas* (p.48) and *pakoras/bhajias* (p.47).

I N G R E D I E N T S

2 tablespoons fresh cilantro/coriander leaves, chopped

1 tablespoon fresh mint leaves, chopped

1 clove garlic, crushed

1 green chili, finely chopped or ground

1 tablespoon lemon juice

1 tablespoon yogurt or thick coconut milk

salt

Put all the ingredients into a blender and whizz for a few seconds to mix well. Add more yogurt or coconut milk as desired to make the consistency you prefer ∎

INDIA

Imli chutney (Tamarind chutney)

This is quite a sour chutney which contrasts well with onion *bhajias* and other fried snacks.

I N G R E D I E N T S

1 tablespoon / 50 g pressed tamarind

3 dried dates, stoned and chopped +

$^{1}/_{2}$ cup / 120 ml water

$^{1}/_{4}$ teaspoon ground cumin

$^{1}/_{4}$ teaspoon chili powder

$^{1}/_{2}$-1 tablespoon sugar

salt

+ optional ingredient

1. Simmer the tamarind and dates in the water for about 5-7 minutes.

2. Now agitate the tamarind to help loosen the pulp. Remove the tamarind and dates from the water and place them in a sieve above the bowl. Press with wooden spoon to force the pulp through, leaving the tamarind seeds behind.

3. Next, toast the ground cumin for a minute or two in a small pan without any oil, stirring it round until it darkens a little.

4. When this is done, place all the ingredients in a bowl and mix well or use a blender ∎

SRI LANKA

Tomato chutney

'Over 2,500 years, Sri Lanka has had trading links with Indians, Arabs, Chinese and Malays and has absorbed some of their culture and cuisine. Later came the colonizing Portuguese, Dutch and British who also left their mark.

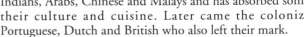

'This chutney is a fine chaser with noodles or plain rice and would serve even as a sauce that is not blatantly hot on the palate. Note that the chili needs to soak in the vinegar for about two hours.' *Nalin Wijesekera, Mount Lavinia, Sri Lanka*

I N G R E D I E N T S

1 cup / 240 ml vinegar

2 dried red chilis, soaked in the vinegar for 2 hours

2 cloves garlic, crushed

$^1/_2$ teaspoon fresh ginger, grated

2 tablespoons sugar or to taste

1 pound / 450 g tomatoes, sliced

$^1/_2$ cup / 50 g dates, stoned and chopped

salt

FOR THE SPICE POWDER (1 TEASPOON) – CRUSH THESE AND MIX TOGETHER

2 cloves

seeds from 5 cardamom pods

$^1/_2$-inch / 1.5-cm piece of cinnamon

1. Remove the chilis from the vinegar, retaining this for later use. Grind the soaked chilis with the ginger and garlic in a blender.

2. Now put the vinegar, sugar and salt into a large pan and bring to the boil.

3. At this point, add the tomatoes, dates and the teaspoon of spice powder. Stir them round and then simmer on a moderate heat until the mixture becomes very thick and has the consistency you like for chutney.

4. Remove the pan from the heat, allow to cool a little and then spoon the chutney into warmed jars. Cover and once opened, store in the refrigerator for up to 6 weeks ■

Curd sambal

'The staple food of Sri Lanka, rice and curry, has many versions – the rice tempered with *ghee* (clarified butter), spiced, cooked in stock or coconut milk. Some of the accompanying *sambals* (like this one), *fricadells*, *lamprais*, *breudher*, or *kokis* proclaim their Portuguese and Dutch origins.' *Nalin Wijesekera, Mount Lavinia, Sri Lanka*

I N G R E D I E N T S

1 cucumber, thinly sliced

2 cups / 440 g yogurt

$^1/_2$ onion, very finely sliced

1 green chili, finely chopped +

salt

+ optional ingredient

1. Put the cucumber slices on a plate and sprinkle them with salt. Leave for 1 hour in the refrigerator.

2. After this, squeeze out the salty liquid. Then place the cucumber in a bowl and spoon in the yogurt, onion and chili. Combine these ingredients and serve ■

NOODLES

ANY years ago, BBC TV screened a report from Italy on its flagship program, Panorama. Presented by Richard Dimbleby, viewers saw orchards of trees bearing swathes of long spaghetti noodles from their branches, and heard about the prospects for the harvest.

It was fascinating, but surely...? Yes, finally the gullible realized they had been hoodwinked. The very proper BBC had played an April Fool joke on its viewers, and delighted them. Maybe today it would be impossible to fool anybody in this way. For one thing, we know not to believe everything we see on TV. But also, pasta and noodles are more familiar to us now.

While pasta is associated with Italy and noodles with China, they are eaten in many parts of the world. As to which developed first, it is hard to say. Marco Polo, credited with 'discovering' noodles in 13th century China is now thought to have reported simply that he had found noodles 'like ours'. Whatever the truth, both places have been producing pasta and noodles for thousands of years. Macaroni in Italy dates back to Etruscan times, and there were noodles about three thousand years ago in China, where they were invented by ordinary people (though soon even the Emperor was eating them).

Noodles are made from wheat, rice or buckwheat flour as well as from pea or bean starch. And it is amazing what can be done with such simple ingredients.

In Italy there are shapes and sizes enough to dizzy the imagination – from *spaghetti* ('string') or *rotini* (spirals) to ribbon-shaped egg noodles called *tagliatelle* or *fettucine*. Then there are *capelletti* ('little hats'), like *ravioli*, and the thin *vermicelli* or 'little worms'. And that is just a few. Other European countries have pasta too – *tarhonya* from Hungary, shaped like barley grains; the Greeks have their rice-shaped *manestra*; while in Jewish cookery noodles feature in items like *kugel* pudding.

Arabs, Persians and Indians had also been enjoying pasta from early times. These are known as *reshta* or *rishta* ('thread') in Arabic, and in Morocco there is a thin short variety called *sheriya*. In India, *sevika*, *seviyan* and *sev* are names of the noodles – again meaning 'thread'. Very fine wheat or potato flour vermicelli type noodles, they are mostly used for milk desserts.

Over in South America, noodles are found too – probably a result of the Arab/Moorish influence on Spanish cuisine. Mexican *fideos* are popular in soups.

There is an abundance of Asian noodles, bearing different names and prepared in different ways. There are the intriguing 'cellophane' noodles made of mung-bean flour – transparent as their name suggests, and used in many Thai, Cambodian, Laotian, Burmese and Filipino dishes as well as in China, where they go by the pleasant name of *fun see*. Buckwheat *soba* noodles crop up in Japan and Korea.

There are noodles made of seaweed; also big flat rice noodles and vermicelli types. There are shoe-lace noodles made of wheat flour with egg, and ones without egg called *main fun* in China.

Pho is the name for a Vietnamese anytime noodle soup, while a popular dish in China and Malaysia is birthday *mee* – served on someone's birthday of course – long wheat noodles served with a rice sauce. The long strands symbolize longevity, and woe betide you if you break them as you chopstick them up to your mouth ∎

SOUTH PACIFIC/ASIA

Coconut milk

An essential ingredient in many dishes around the world, coconut milk gives a fragrance and richness to foods. It is increasingly easy to buy in various forms.

Remember when cooking with coconut milk to stir the dish as it comes to the boil. The pan should not be covered during cooking as the milk may curdle.

Canned – Stir the tin on opening to mix the contents well. Use in recipes calling for just 'coconut milk'.

Some recipes require thin and thick coconut milk. For this, buy two cans of $1^1/_4$ cups/300 ml each. To make the thin coconut milk, open one can and scoop off the thick cream at the top. Set this aside. Pour the remaining liquid into a measuring jug to make the quantity you require. For the thick coconut milk, open the second can and stir well. Add the cream from the first can.

Creamed – For one cup put $^1/_2$ cup/100 g into a bowl and gradually pour in $^2/_3$ cup/150 ml of hot water. Mix well. This is suitable for any recipes needing 'coconut milk' or 'thick coconut milk'.

If 'thin coconut milk' is called for, put $^1/_2$ cup/75 g into a bowl and add $1^1/_4$ cups/300 ml of hot water; this should make about $1^1/_2$ cups/350 ml of thin coconut milk.

Powdered – This is very easy to use. For thick coconut milk put 2-3 tablespoons of the powder into a jug or bowl and add 1 cup/240 ml warm water to make a creamy liquid. For a thinner milk, use 1 tablespoon of powder with the same amount of water. Pour into the food you are cooking, stirring as you do so.

Dried / Desiccated

2 cups / 150 g dried/desiccated coconut
$2^1/_2$ cups / 590 ml boiling water

1. Soak the coconut in boiling water and then leave it to cool a little.
2. When this is done, blend the mixture together until it becomes a smooth paste. You can use it like this, or else squeeze the mixture through a piece of muslin or a fine sieve to remove any bits.

3. Where a recipe specifies 'thick' and 'thin' coconut milk, this will do as an all-purpose substitute.

Fresh – Punch 2 holes in the end of the coconut with 3 indentations, using a screwdriver or other strong implement (not a knife which will bend). One hole is to let the liquid out, the other to let the air in so that the liquid can flow.

Now crack the coconut open by hitting it around the centre with the claw end of a hammer. It should open in 2 halves. Remove the coconut flesh with a knife; if it is reluctant, hold the shells cut side up over a low flame for a few moments, turning them round. This makes the woody shell contract and releases the flesh.

When you have prised off the white part, remove any brown skin with a potato peeler. Now break into 1 inch/2.5 cms pieces or larger if you are going to use a manual grater. Grate or blend. You can freeze this, and indeed some stores now sell frozen grated coconut.

Or you can simply smash the coconut against a rock outside. It will crack, you can catch the liquid if you are quick. Then break the coconut into pieces and leave them aside for a few hours. This slight dehydration will make it easier to prise off the flesh and proceed as in the instructions.

2 cups / 450 g grated coconut
$1^1/_4$ cups / 300 ml hot water

1. Put coconut and water into a blender and blend for a few moments.

2. Then line a sieve with muslin or cheesecloth and stand it over a bowl. Empty the blender contents into it and then gather the ends of the cloth together and squeeze all the liquid out. This makes about $1^1/_2$ cups/350 ml thick coconut milk. Keep the residue to make thin coconut milk.

3. To do this, add very hot water to the coconut pieces and squeeze out the juice. Repeat until you have the quantity you require ∎

BRAZIL

Tutu of black beans

Serves 4

The first Portuguese colonial outposts in Brazil were set up in the early 16th century along the coast, trading brazilwood which was used as a dye by the European textile industry. Brazilwood trade was succeeded by sugar cane cultivation, at first using local Indians for labor. However so many fled and/or succumbed to European diseases that the Portuguese decided to ship in African slaves – thought to be tougher. I have found no clear origin of the intriguing name for this dish ('tutu').

INGREDIENTS

1 cup / 225 g black kidney beans, cooked

2 tablespoons flour

water

1 bayleaf

1/4 teaspoon chili powder

salt and pepper

FOR THE TOPPING

1 onion, chopped

1 bell pepper, thinly sliced

1/2 chili, finely chopped

2 tomatoes, sliced

1 tablespoon fresh cilantro/coriander leaves, chopped

oil

salt and pepper

Heat oven to 350°F/180°C/Gas 4

1. Place the cooked beans in a blender or bowl and mash them using a fork. Transfer them to a saucepan.

2. Sift the flour into a bowl and pour in enough water to make a runny paste. Add this to the beans, together with the bayleaf, chili powder, and seasoning.

3. Now warm up the mixture very slowly, stirring from time to time, until it forms a smooth paste. Let this cook for 5 minutes and then transfer to an ovenproof dish.

4. To prepare the topping, heat the oil and gently cook the onion, bell pepper and chili for a few minutes. Add the tomatoes and half the cilantro/coriander leaves and cook for a further few minutes.

5. Spoon the topping onto the bean mixture and bake in the oven for 10 minutes. Garnish with the remaining cilantro/coriander leaves before serving ∎

CARIBBEAN

Salade à la Caraibe (Caribbean salad)

Serves 4

As the name of this recipe indicates, there is a French legacy in the Caribbean. All the early European colonizing countries had a stake in the islands at one time or another. The US Virgin Islands, for instance, were visited by Columbus in 1493; they were settled by the French and English in the 17th century; then changed hands between British, French and Spanish. Even the Knights of Malta got in on the action until the Danes took over. The islands were sold to the United States in 1917, for $25 million.

INGREDIENTS

1 cup / 110 g white cabbage, shredded

1 cup / 100 g cucumber, grated

1 red bell pepper, finely sliced in circles

1 mango, peeled, stoned and sliced

4-6 scallions/spring onions, chopped

1/2-1 avocado pear, peeled and sliced

1 clove garlic, crushed

juice of 1-2 limes or lemons

4-6 tablespoons olive oil

1 handful watercress

salt and pepper

1. First, arrange the cabbage, cucumber, bell pepper, mango

and scallions/spring onions in a salad bowl.

2. Now put in half the avocado slices.

3. Then blend the garlic with the lime or lemon juice, olive oil and salt and pepper. Pour half the dressing over and toss the salad.

4. Now arrange the cress and remaining avocado slices on top and drizzle the rest of the dressing over before serving ∎

CHILE

Coliflor en salsa de almendra (Cauliflower in almond sauce)

Serves 4-6

Although the repression of the Pinochet dictatorship is over, Chileans face economic hardship. Copper, the main export, is subject to the vagaries of world market prices. Fruit, fishmeal and timber are other exports while food crops are oats, barley, rice, beans, lentils, corn/maize and chickpeas.

This is a flavorsome way to treat that useful standby, the cauliflower. You can also try the sauce using walnuts instead of almonds.

I N G R E D I E N T S

1 cauliflower

1 tablespoon margarine

2 tablespoons flour

3 tablespoons ground almonds

1³/₄ cups / 420 ml milk

1 tablespoon almonds, chopped

1/2 teaspoon nutmeg

1/2 red bell pepper, sliced +

pinch of paprika

1 tablespoon fresh parsley, chopped

4-6 almonds, chopped, for garnish

salt and pepper

+ optional ingredient

1. Trim the cauliflower and make a cross in the bottom of the stem so that the center cooks as quickly as the florets.

2. Boil some salted water in a large enough pan to accommodate the cauliflower (whole) and then cook it, stalk downwards, for 15 minutes, or until it is just tender. Drain and then place in a round serving dish and set aside to keep warm while you make the sauce.

3. For the sauce, melt the margarine in a pan and stir in the flour to make a paste. Cook this for a couple of minutes over a low heat. Now shake in the ground almonds and mix everything together.

4. Remove the pan from the heat and very slowly pour in the milk, stirring as you start to make the sauce smooth. When this is done, return the pan to the heat and sprinkle in the chopped almonds, nutmeg and seasoning.

5. Bring the sauce to the boil, stirring constantly. Add more milk if necessary to achieve the desired consistency – it should be thick enough to coat the cauliflower.

6. Let the sauce simmer for a few minutes to combine the flavors. Then mask the cauliflower with the sauce and serve at once, with the red bell pepper slices, paprika, parsley and a few chopped almonds scattered over the top ∎

GUATEMALA

Tortillas

Makes 12

Tortillas are unique among breads in that they are made from a flour which is already cooked – the corn/maize flour called *masa harina*. Dried corn is boiled with lime until the skins loosen and the cooked, skinned kernels are then dried and ground to make the *masa* dough flour used for tortillas.

This recipe uses a mixture of wheat flour and fine corn/maize meal instead, although you may be able to find *masa harina* where you are. Alternatively use ready-made taco shells or frozen tortillas.

INGREDIENTS

1 cup / 110 g fine corn/maize meal

1 cup / 110 g flour

200 ml warm water

2 pieces of waxed/greaseproof paper or aluminium foil, cut into 8-inch/20-cm squares *

* Using greased paper or foil enables you to roll the sticky dough into a very thin pancake. In Central America, a special tortilla press is often used for this.

1. Place the corn/maize meal and flour in a bowl and pour in enough water to make a dough. Knead well until it is elastic and then divide it into 12 pieces.

2. Grease the paper or foil sheets next. Now put one of the lumps of dough in the centre of a sheet, place the second sheet on top and use a rolling pin to make a 6-inch/15-cm circle.

3. When this is ready, heat a lightly-greased shallow pan or griddle. Peel away one layer of paper or foil from the tortilla and place the pancake in the pan or griddle with the second sheet of paper or foil still in place on the upper side.

4. Cook for about 1 minute and then remove the paper or foil and turn the tortilla over to cook the second side. Both sides should be dry with brown patches.

5. Stack the tortillas and keep them warm. They may become brittle if cooled and are best eaten as soon as possible after cooking ■

MARTINIQUE

Colombo de giraumon (Spicy pumpkin)

Serves 4

The name Martinique may derive from 'Martinica' after St Martin, or from the island's Indian name 'Madinina'. The French settled it in 1635 and in 1763 Marie-Josephe Tascher de la Pagerie was born here, later to be Empress Josephine to Napoleon.

If you cannot find pumpkin, try this recipe with sweet potatoes.

I N G R E D I E N T S

1 onion, finely sliced

1-2 cloves garlic, crushed

2 teaspoons curry powder

3 cloves, crushed

$^1/_2$ red chili, finely chopped

1 pound / 450 g pumpkin, peeled and cut into 1-inch/ 2.5-cm cubes

2 tomatoes, chopped

1 tablespoon sultanas

$^1/_4$ teaspoon sugar +

juice of 1 lemon

2 tablespoons oil

salt and pepper

+ optional ingredient

1. First, heat the oil in a heavy pan and then add the onion. Sauté until it is transparent and then add the garlic and cook that also.

2. Next put in the curry powder, ground cloves and chili and cook for a further 2 minutes.

3. When this is done, add the pumpkin chunks, the chopped tomatoes, the sultanas and sugar. Sprinkle the lemon juice over.

4. Cover, and cook very gently for 30-40 minutes or until the pumpkin is tender, stirring frequently to ensure that it does not catch. Season and serve to accompany main dishes and rice ∎

MEXICO

Berros salad

Serves 4-6

'Like the *pico de gallo* relish (p.130), this salad contains the colors of Mexico's national flag: green, white and red. Green for the forests, white for the snow-capped volcanoes and red for the blood of the heroes of the independence struggle.

'The salad should stand for at least 2 hours before serving so that the dressing takes the edge off the pungent radishes.'
Caitlin Buck and José Andrés Christen, Leeds, UK, and Mexico

I N G R E D I E N T S

$^1/_2$ pound / 225 g watercress

10 red radishes, topped and tailed

4-6 tablespoons olive oil

2 tablespoons vinegar

salt

1. Separate out the watercress strands and place them in a salad bowl.

2. Cut the radishes into thin, round slices and then mix most of them in with the watercress, retaining some for a garnish.

3. Now join the olive oil to the vinegar and mix well with the salad, adding salt. Decorate with the remaining radish slices before placing in the refrigerator for about 2 hours until required ∎

Pico de gallo (Chili relish or chutney)

About half of Mexico's cultivable land is held by the *ejidos*, rural communities that farm small individual or collective lots. Corn/maize is the principal cereal with beans and potatoes also grown. Drought and lack of subsidies and inputs all depress production. The large commercial farms of the northwest produce coffee, cotton, fresh fruit, sugar, tobacco and tomatoes, mainly for export.

This should stand for at least one hour before serving. Its piquancy complements bland dishes such as *frijoles refritos* (p.88) and *molletes* (p.93).

I N G R E D I E N T S

1 onion, finely chopped

2-3 tomatoes, finely sliced

2 tablespoons fresh cilantro/coriander leaves or parsley, chopped

1-2 chilis, finely chopped

juice of 2 limes or lemons

salt

1. Mix all the ingredients together in a salad bowl. Sprinkle with salt and cover with the lime or lemon juice.

2. Set aside to stand for 1 hour, turning from time to time, and then serve ∎

PARAGUAY

Sopa Paraguaya (Paraguayan corn bread)

Serves 4

Pre-Columbian people in the Americas made flat breads such as *arepas* and *tortillas* out of corn/maize meal. When the Europeans came, other breads evolved such as this one which incorporates cheese and makes a tasty and substantial accompaniment to salads and main dishes.

I N G R E D I E N T S

1 can creamed corn kernels

$^1/_2$ cup / 75 g corn/maize meal

$^2/_3$ cup / 150 ml milk

2 cups / 200 g cheddar or monterrey jack cheese, grated

1 onion, finely chopped

3 eggs

1 tablespoon flour

1 tablespoon butter or margarine

4 tablespoons oil

salt

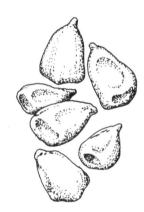

Heat oven to 400°F/200°C/Gas 6

1. First, grease a 8-inch/20-cm square baking tin or dish. Sprinkle on some flour and then tap the tin to remove the excess.

2. Now put the corn kernels into a bowl with the corn/maize meal, milk, cheese and a little salt. Add 3 tablespoons of the oil and mix everything well.

3. Next heat up the remaining tablespoon of oil in a pan and sauté the onion; then add this to the corn mixture.

4. When this is done, separate the eggs and whisk the whites until they are stiff. Now beat the yolks and gently fold them into the whites.

5. Spoon the blended eggs into the corn mixture and then pour this into the baking dish and dot with butter or margarine. Bake for about 45 minutes ∎

GULF STATES/IRAQ

Roz bil tamar (Rice with dates and almonds)

Serves 4

Rice with dates in some combination is a staple food both of the nomadic Bedouin and urbanites alike. Rose water can be obtained in Indian or other specialist grocery stores, but if you cannot find it then use a little grated orange peel instead to give the dish fragrance.

I N G R E D I E N T S

1 cup / 125 g almonds

1 cup / 100 g dates, stoned

1 cup / 100 g sultanas or raisins

1 teaspoon rose water or a little grated orange rind

1 cup / 225 g rice, cooked

2 tablespoons margarine

salt

1. Melt the margarine in a large pan and when it is gently bubbling, add the almonds. Fry them, stirring often, for one or two minutes.

2. Next put in the dates and sultanas or raisins, adding more margarine if necessary. Keep stirring so that nothing sticks or burns, and cook for a few minutes until the dried fruit begins to plump up.

3. Now heap the rice on top of the fruit and nut mixture;

cover. Cook over a very gentle heat, or place in a low oven, for 10–20 minutes to let everything heat through.

4. Just before serving, sprinkle on the rose water and garnish with additional almonds and orange peel ∎

IRAN

Borani esfanaj (Spinach and yogurt salad)

Serves 4

'Iran' comes from the word 'Ayriana'. In Sanskrit this means 'nobles' which explains why Hitler used the word 'Aryan' to describe the super-race he wanted to create in Germany, in part his response to the humiliation of Germany's First World War defeat.

War has frequently touched Iran too, both directly in the 1980–1988 conflict with Iraq and indirectly with the fighting in Afghanistan and the Gulf. In 1992, Iran had the world's second largest refugee population with two million Afghanis, and more than a million Iraqi Kurds also fled there after the Gulf War.

I N G R E D I E N T S

1 onion, finely chopped

2 cloves garlic, crushed

1 pound / 450 g spinach, chopped

1 cup / 225 g yogurt

2 tablespoons oil

salt and pepper

1. Heat the oil and sauté the onion for several minutes until it is golden. Then add the garlic and after a minute or two, put in the spinach and seasoning.

2. Cook the spinach, turning from time to time, until it has settled and softened. Transfer it to a serving dish and let it cool.

3. When ready to serve, blend in the yogurt and mix well ∎

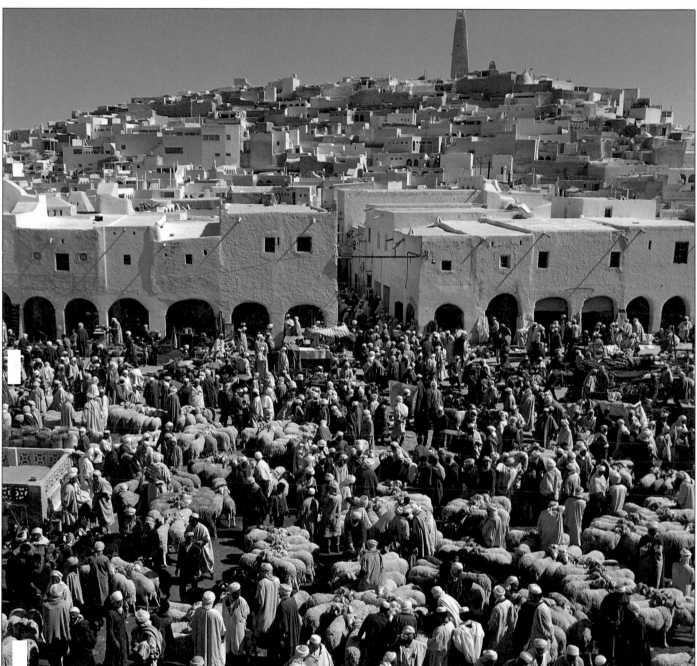

Market for the festival of Eid, Ghardia, Algeria. *Photo: John Wright/Hutchison Photo Library.*

LEBANON

Tabbouli (Bulghur wheat salad)

Serves 4-6

Bulghur or *bulghul* is made from wheat which has been boiled and dried and then ground. It needs no cooking - you simply soak the grains for about 20 minutes before using. It can be bought from health food stores. *Tabbouli* can be served as a starter (one of a range of *mezze*) or as an accompanying salad.

I N G R E D I E N T S

¹/₂ cup / 110 g bulghur

a few lettuce leaves

4 tablespoons fresh parsley, chopped

2 tablespoons fresh mint, chopped

1 onion, finely sliced

4 tomatoes, chopped

4 tablespoons lemon juice

4 tablespoons olive oil

salt and pepper

1. First, soak the bulghur for 20 minutes or so in enough cold water to cover. Then drain well.

2. Line a salad bowl with the lettuce leaves and then spoon in the bulghur. Scatter in 3 tablespoons of the parsley together with the mint, onion and tomatoes and mix them in.

3. Now join the lemon juice to the oil, season with salt and pepper and mix well. Pour this over and toss the salad to coat the ingredients evenly. Sprinkle the remaining spoonful of parsley on top ■

Fava or broad bean salad

Serves 4

Lebanon's ancient history is bound up with Syria, of which it was part. In 1916 France took control of Syria and Lebanon and separated them. Muslim/Christian antagonism has been part of the country's recent history. Beirut, once a key political and cultural center in the Arab world, has been virtually destroyed.

I N G R E D I E N T S

1 pound / 450 g broad beans (canned or frozen will do)

2 cloves garlic, crushed

¹/₂ teaspoon chili powder

juice of ¹/₂ lemon

1 tablespoon fresh parsley, chopped

2 tablespoons olive oil

salt

1. If using fresh or frozen beans, put them into a saucepan containing boiling water and cook for a few minutes until tender; drain.

2. Now mix the garlic and chili powder in a bowl together with the salt. Add the beans to this mixture and mash them with a fork or use a blender. Combine all the ingredients well and transfer to a small shallow dish.

3. Combine the lemon juice and olive oil and pour over; scatter the fresh parsley on top. Serve with hot pitta bread ■

```
IN ALL RECIPES
● PEPPER AND SALT ARE TO TASTE.
● CHILI AND SUGAR ARE GIVEN AS GUIDE QUANTITIES ONLY.
VARY TO TASTE.
● MEASURES FOR BEANS AND GRAINS REFER TO DRY INGREDIENTS.
```

MIDDLE EAST

Fasolyeh bi ban banadoora (Beans with tomatoes)

Serves 4

Allspice, used here, is so called because it combines the flavor of several spices. Known also as *pimento*, it comes from the dried unripe fruits of a small evergreen tree found in the Caribbean and Central America.

This is a typical dish from the region which can be varied using other vegetables such as peas, carrots and broad beans.

I N G R E D I E N T S

1 onion, finely sliced

1 pound / 450 g green beans (French, runner or string beans), cut into 1-inch/2.5-cm pieces

$^1/_2$ teaspoon allspice

$^1/_2$ teaspoon ground cumin

2-3 tomatoes, chopped

1 cup / 225 g yogurt

2 tablespoons oil

salt and pepper

1. Heat the oil and sauté the onion. Then put in the beans, allspice, cumin and seasoning. Reduce the heat, cover the pan and cook for 5 minutes or so.

2. After this, remove the cover and throw in the tomatoes. Continue to cook until they are tender. Serve with yogurt ■

TUNISIA

Zucchini/courgette salad

Serves 4-6

The caraway plant is found from Europe to the Himalayas and its aromatic seeds have been used since early times, both medicinally as a remedy for flatulence, and as flavoring for bread, cakes, soups and the liqueur, *Kümmel*. Caraway seeds are sometimes confused with cumin because they look similar, but their taste is different and they should not be used interchangeably. In Sweden, caraway is called *kummin* which may help explain the confusion.

To let the flavors expand, leave this salad to stand for an hour before serving.

I N G R E D I E N T S

1 pound / 450 g zucchini/courgettes, sliced

4-6 tablespoons olive oil

2-3 tablespoons lemon juice

2 cloves garlic, crushed

1 teaspoon caraway seeds, crushed

pinch of paprika

salt and pepper

1. Steam the zucchini/courgettes or boil them in a little salted water.

2. While they are cooking, join the olive oil to the lemon

juice. Mix well and then add the garlic, caraway seeds, and also the salt and pepper.

3. Drain the zucchini/courgettes and place them in a serving dish. Pour the dressing over, mix well, and sprinkle a little paprika on top before serving as it is, or cold ∎

Bell pepper and cucumber salad

Serves 4

Wheat, barley, corn/maize, sorghum, olives, dates and citrus fruit make up some of the food crops in Tunisia, but fewer and fewer people now work on the land. Forty per cent of Tunisia's population is under 15 years old and seem destined to head for the growing manufacturing sector, or to try their luck abroad as migrant workers.

INGREDIENTS

a few lettuce leaves

6 inches / 15 cms cucumber, thinly sliced

1 green bell pepper, sliced in circles

2 tomatoes, sliced

$1/2$ onion, thinly sliced in circles

4 tablespoons oil

1 tablespoon vinegar

1 tablespoon lemon juice

a dash of sugar

$1/4$ teaspoon dry mustard

$1/4$ teaspoon paprika

salt and pepper

1. Taking a shallow serving plate or dish, arrange the lettuce leaves to make the base of the salad.

2. Then arrange the slices of cucumber, bell pepper, tomato and onion in overlapping layers or as liked.

3. Finally, combine the oil with the vinegar and lemon juice. Add the sugar, mustard, paprika and salt and pepper and pour the dressing over the vegetables ∎

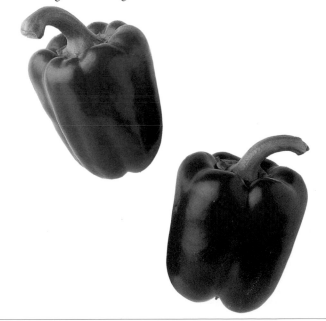

TUNISIA

Salade de zalouk (Spicy vegetable salad)

Serves 4

Tunisia's French connection shows in this salad's title. The French invaded in 1882 under an arrangement with the British, to compensate for France's loss of the Suez canal. The country gained independence in 1956. Today, Islamic influence is on the rise and the University of the Koran was reopened in the late 1980s.

INGREDIENTS

¹/₂ teaspoon chili powder

2 cloves garlic, crushed

1 egg-plant/aubergine, cut into cubes

2 zucchini/courgettes, sliced

2 red or green bell peppers, sliced

4 tomatoes, chopped

¹/₂ chili, chopped

4 tablespoons oil

salt and pepper

1. First heat the oil and put in the chili powder, garlic and a little salt.

2. Next, sauté the egg-plant/aubergine cubes for a few minutes, followed by the zucchini/courgettes and then the bell peppers.

3. Add the tomatoes and chili now and cook without the lid, stirring frequently, until all the vegetables have amalgamated and most of the liquid has evaporated.

4. Check the flavors and seasoning and adjust to taste. Transfer the salad to a bowl and allow to cool before serving ∎

DESSERTS

Girl with bananas at the Damnam Saduak floating market, Thailand. *Photo: Mervyn Rees/Tory Stone Worldwide.*

CAMEROON

Banana bread

Bananas are a main cash (export) crop in Cameroon along with cocoa, coffee, cotton, tobacco, rubber, palm oil and sugar. Tropical wood is another major source of income, and although the country is about 40 per cent forested it will not remain so for much longer.

This popular cake turns up all over the world where bananas grow (and even in places where they don't). A Caribbean version would likely add cinnamon, walnuts and dried fruit such as sultanas. There is also a Ghanaian cake, *ablongo*, that uses plantains (cooking bananas) and the distinctively-flavored red palm oil.

I N G R E D I E N T S

1³/₄ cups / 225 g flour

1 teaspoon soda bicarbonate

1 teaspoon baking powder

2 tablespoons margarine

¹/₃ cup / 75 g sugar

2 eggs, beaten

3 ripe bananas, mashed

salt

Heat oven to 350°F/180°C/Gas 4

1. Sift the flour together with the bicarbonate of soda, baking powder and a little salt into a bowl.

2. In another bowl, cream the margarine with the sugar and then add the beaten eggs, a little at a time. If the mixture curdles, put in some of the flour and mix well.

3. The mashed bananas and the flour can go in now; stir well.

4. Next, grease a loaf tin and spoon in the mixture. Bake for about 1 hour or until done – test by piercing with a kebab skewer or knitting needle. It should come out clean.

5. Remove the bread from the oven but leave it to stand in the tin for 15 minutes. Then turn it out to cool on a rack. If possible, leave until the next day before serving, cut into slices spread with margarine if liked ∎

GUINEA

Docono (Semolina dessert)
Serves 2-4

Lying on West Africa's coast, Guinea is flanked by Guinea-Bissau, Senegal, Mali, Côte d'Ivoire, Liberia and Sierra Leone. Its economy relies on bauxite, used for aluminium. About 80 per cent of the people are subsistence farmers, growing rice, cassava/manioc, corn/maize and vegetables, plus bananas, groundnuts, pineapples and coffee for export.

This dessert may strike a familiar note; semolina was one of the range of 'milk puddings' habitually eaten by schoolchildren in Britain to build them up. Other versions used sago, rice and tapioca – all imported from Britain's colonies.

INGREDIENTS

3 tablespoons semolina

1-2 tablespoons sugar

2¹/₂ cups / 590 ml milk

¹/₂ teaspoon vanilla essence

¹/₂ teaspoon cinnamon

2 bananas, sliced

1. Place the semolina in a mixing bowl together with the sugar and pour in enough cold milk to make a paste.

2. Now put the rest of the milk on to boil. When it reaches boiling point, pour it into the semolina paste, a little at a time, stirring constantly so that the mixture is smooth.

3. Return this now to the saucepan and bring it to the boil, stirring frequently to prevent catching.

4. Let the semolina simmer for 5-10 minutes and then take it from the heat and stir in the vanilla essence, cinnamon and sliced bananas. Serve at once, or leave it to cool ■

MALAWI

Mbatata pudding (Sweet potato pudding)

Serves 2-4

Farming is the main source of livelihood for Malawians, both as small-holders growing corn/maize and groundnuts, and also as estate farmers producing tobacco, sugar and tea for export. Local industry produces textiles, cigarettes, beer, sugar, some pharmaceuticals and cement. As a result of the war in Mozambique, Malawi hosted nearly one million refugees.

INGREDIENTS

2 sweet potatoes, chopped

2-3 teaspoons honey

1 tablespoon sherry or brandy +

2 tablespoons margarine

1 egg, separated

rind and juice of an orange

+ optional ingredient

Heat oven to 400°F/200°C/Gas 6

1. Place the sweet potatoes in a saucepan of boiling water and cook until they are soft, about 10 minutes. Drain and then put them into a bowl and mash them.

2. Now add all the other ingredients, except the egg white, and mix them together.

3. When this is done, whisk the egg white until it is stiff and then fold it into the mixture.

4. Grease an ovenproof dish and spoon in the pudding. Bake until golden brown, about 45 minutes-1 hour ■

Women pounding grain, West Africa. *Photo: Claude Sauvageot.*

SOUTH AFRICA

Melktert (Milk tart)

Serves 4-6

This Afrikaner dessert appears in coffee shops and restaurants and is also served as a mid-morning or tea-time snack. With its use of cinnamon, *melktert* shows the influence of the Afrikaners' forebears at the Cape, the Dutch, and their spice trade with what is now Indonesia. In their determination to monopolize this trade, the Dutch burned down the spice trees from time to time, to keep prices high in Europe.

I N G R E D I E N T S

¹/₂ pound / 225 g frozen pastry, thawed

2 eggs, separated

2¹/₂ cups / 590 ml milk

2¹/₂ tablespoons cornstarch/cornflour

2 tablespoons sugar

piece of cinnamon

¹/₂ teaspoon cinnamon powder

Heat oven to 425°F/220°C/Gas 7

1. Roll out the pastry extremely thinly and then line a 8-inch/20-cm pie dish with it. Cut a circle of waxed/greaseproof paper, place this on the pastry and weight it with some dried beans. Bake the pastry-case for 8-10 minutes and then remove it from the oven and set aside.

2. Turn down the oven to 325°F/160°C/Gas 3.

3. Separate the eggs and beat the yolks with the sugar.

4. Spoon the cornstarch/cornflour into a small bowl and add a little of the milk to make a smooth paste. Set the rest of the milk on to boil, and toss in the stick of cinnamon.

5. When the milk is at boiling point, pour some back into the cornstarch/cornflour mixture and blend thoroughly. Then return this to the saucepan containing the milk.

6. Bring to the boil gently, stirring all the time as it thickens. When it is creamy, remove from the heat and set aside to cool a little, stirring from time to time to prevent skin forming. Take out the piece of cinnamon.

7. When the milk is cool, add the beaten yolk and sugar mixture. Now whisk the egg whites until they are stiff and then fold these in. Stir everything together so that it mingles and then spoon it into the waiting pie case.

8. Sprinkle a little cinnamon powder and sugar if liked on the top and bake the pie for 1 hour or until set – firm to the touch and not wobbly when you gently shake the dish. Serve cool or cold ■

> **IN ALL RECIPES**
> ● **PEPPER AND SALT ARE TO TASTE.**
> ● **CHILI AND SUGAR ARE GIVEN AS GUIDE QUANTITIES ONLY.**
> **VARY TO TASTE.**
> ● **MEASURES FOR BEANS AND GRAINS REFER TO DRY INGREDIENTS.**

BANGLADESH

Mal pua (Coconut pancakes)

Makes about 15 small pancakes

'*Agrahayan* is the harvest season in Bangladesh, and this is also the time when Bengali kitchens emit the delicious aromas of *pithas* (homemade pancakes) being cooked. The main ingredients are usually the newly-harvested rice ground into a paste and blended with molasses from date palms.

'The recipe that follows is more simple, while still using one of the most popular ingredients for Bengali sweet lovers: the coconut. You can omit the syrup if desired and the pancakes are best cooked in a *korai* (wok).' *Meghna Guhathakurta, Dhaka, Bangladesh*

INGREDIENTS

1 cup / 75 g dried/desiccated coconut

1 cup / 110 g rice flour or wheat flour

1 cup / 240 ml milk

1-2 tablespoons sugar

seeds from 1 cardamom pod, crushed

oil

FOR THE SYRUP +

1 cup / 240 ml water

1 cup / 225 g sugar

+ optional

1. In a bowl, mix the coconut, flour and milk together to make a runny paste, if necessary adding a drop more milk. Then sprinkle in the sugar and cardamom seeds and stir well.

2. Heat enough oil for deep frying in a wok (about 2 inches/5 cms) and when it is very hot, take a spoonful of the mixture and slide it into the oil. It will quickly form a small pancake. Deep-fry on both sides to a golden brown colour.

3. Remove the pancake from the wok and drain on kitchen paper. Keep warm while you cook the rest. Eat as they are, or with honey, or syrup, see below.

4. For the syrup, boil the water and then stir in the sugar. Boil vigorously for 10-20 minutes until the mixture transforms into syrup. Let it cool a bit and then deftly dip in the pancakes before eating at once ■

CHINA

Hsing jen cha (Almond dessert)

Serves 4

Balance in flavors – as well as in textures, cooking methods and colors – is an important part of Chinese cuisine. The Five Flavors are: bitter, salt, sour, hot and sweet and this dessert slips pleasantly into the final category.

The almond, closely related to the peach, became established in central Asia. It spread to the Mediterranean and was taken to North America by European settlers. Note that the rice and almonds need to soak overnight.

INGREDIENTS

³/₄ cup / 200 g pudding rice

³/₄ cup / 100 g almonds

2¹/₂ cups / 590 ml water

4-6 tablespoons sugar

1 teaspoon almond essence or seeds of 1 cardamom pod, crushed

a few shelled pistachios or whole unskinned almonds

1. Drain the rice and almonds and grind them in a blender. Then put the mixture into a heavy pan and pour in the water; bring to the boil.

2. Cook very gently for 30 minutes, stirring frequently.

3. When the rice is ready, add the sugar and the almond essence and stir well until the sugar dissolves and the flavors have fused. Decorate with pistachios or whole, unskinned almonds ■

INDIA

Aam ras (Mango dessert)

Serves 4

'*Aam ras* is a favorite in Gujerat in the mango season – though Gujeratis would probably be shocked at the idea of using Alphonsos (the best mangoes) to make it. However as the mangoes in Western supermarkets are quite unlike Indian

varieties, a can of Alphonso comes in handy. Other canned varieties, or fresh mangoes of course can be used instead. In Gujerat sweets are eaten along with the other dishes, or even at the beginning of a meal. *Aam ras* can be frozen and makes a delicious ice-cream.' *Dinyar Godrej, Oxford, UK*

INGREDIENTS

5 cups / 750 g mango pulp

1 cup / 220 ml single cream

seeds of 3 green cardamom pods, crushed

a few strands of saffron infused in a little warm milk +

sugar to taste

+ optional ingredient

1. If using fresh mangoes, remove the skin and slice the fruit into a bowl. Then cut it into very small pieces or put it into a blender.

2. Put the mango pulp, cream, cardamom seeds and saffron if using into a blender and whizz for a few seconds to combine, or mix the ingredients well in a bowl with hand beater or whisk. Chill before serving ■

INDIA

Christmas cake

A legacy of the Raj? Or was this combination of dried fruits, nuts and spices already part of the rich Middle Eastern/north Indian cuisine…? Whatever the answer, this cake with its use of semolina and ginger is distinctive and tastes excellent. It is not as heavy on the stomach as the usual Christmas cakes.

You need to start this cake by soaking the dried fruit in the rum or brandy for at least a week before you want to cook it.

I N G R E D I E N T S

2 cups / 225 g mixed peel

2 cups / 225 g currants

2 cups / 225 g raisins or sultanas

2 cups / 250 g almonds or cashew nuts (or mixed half and half)

1/2 cup / 50 g glacé cherries

1 teaspoon ground mixed spice

1/2 cup / 50 g preserved ginger, finely chopped

1/4 cup / 60 ml rum or brandy

1/2 pound / 225 g semolina

1/2 cup / 60 g self-rising flour

1 1/2 cups / 350 g sugar

1/2 pound / 225 g margarine

6 eggs, separated

1/4 cup / 60 ml milk

1/4 teaspoon salt

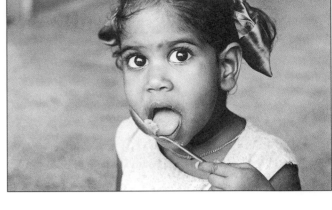

Heat oven to 350°F/180°C/Gas 4

1. Chop the nuts and dried fruit as liked and then put them into a container with a lid and pour the rum or brandy on top. Leave to soak for a week.

2. When ready to make the cake, take a large bowl and cream the margarine with 1 cup/225 g of the sugar to produce a smooth consistency.

3. Beat the egg yolks now and add them a little at a time, stir-ring well. Should the mixture begin to curdle, sift in some of the flour.

4. The rest of the flour goes in now, together with the semolina. Then gradually add the mixture of soaked fruit and nuts and their liquor.

5. Now whisk the egg whites to a stiff froth and fold them into the cake mixture.

6. Next, spoon the remaining sugar into a saucepan. Place on the heat and cook, stirring all the time, until the sugar turns dark brown. When this is done, remove the pan from the heat and pour in the milk, stirring thoroughly. Put in the salt and then empty this mixture into the cake and stir well.

7. Grease a 8-inch/20-cm square cake tin, spoon in the mixture and bake in the middle of the oven for about 1 1/2 hours or until done. Leave the cake to cool in the tin for half an hour before turning it out onto a rack or plate. Store in a tin or container with a tight-fitting lid ■

Carrot halva

Serves 2-4

India ranks as the 15th industrial power in the world, and has its own nuclear industry, arms manufacture and space satellite program. Yet for the majority of people living in the country's half million villages, life has not altered greatly. Over 60 per cent of India's people work in agriculture, with wheat, rice, pulses, tea and potatoes among the main foods grown.

The *halva* can be kept in the fridge for up to a week and is usually re-heated before serving.

INGREDIENTS

1/2 pound / 225 g carrots, grated

4 cardamom pods

1 1/2 cups / 350 ml milk

2 tablespoons ghee or margarine

2-4 tablespoons sugar

1 tablespoon sultanas

1 tablespoon unsalted pistachio nuts, shelled and lightly crushed or use walnuts

1/2 cup / 110 g strained yogurt or thick cream

1. Place the grated carrots with the cardamom pods into a heavy saucepan and pour in the milk.

2. Bring to the boil and then reduce the heat and cook, stirring from time to time, until virtually all the liquid has evaporated – this will take 1/2 hour or more.

3. Now warm the margarine or ghee in a pan and put in the carrot mixture. Stir and fry for 10-15 minutes until the carrots lose their wet milkiness and turn a rich reddish color.

4. At this point, sprinkle in the sugar, sultanas and pistachios or walnuts. Stir-fry for a further 2 minutes and serve with yogurt or cream ■

MALAYSIA

Pisang pancakes (Banana pancakes)

Serves 4

Bananas originally came from south east Asia and they grow there in a range of shapes, tastes and colors. In Malaysia these pancakes might be made from the small 'ladies' fingers' or the red-skinned types, but of course any bananas will do. They are best eaten freshly cooked – but that probably will not be a problem as they tend to get eaten very quickly. Try adding a squeeze of lemon and sugar.

INGREDIENTS

2 eggs

1 tablespoon sugar

1 cup / 125 g self-rising flour

1 tablespoon coconut cream

4-5 bananas, mashed

margarine

1. Begin by beating the eggs with the sugar. Then sift the flour and fold it into the eggs, a little at a time, alternating with pouring in the coconut cream.

2. When that is done, scoop in the mashed bananas and mix well.

3. Melt a little margarine in a fry pan and when it is hot pour in 2 tablespoons of the batter. Tilt the pan so that the pancake mix coats the bottom and cook until lightly brown. Then turn and cook the other side.

4. Fold the pancake into a triangle and remove it from the pan; set aside to keep warm while you cook the others. Serve with wedges of lemon and banana slices ■

IN ALL RECIPES
● **PEPPER AND SALT ARE TO TASTE.**
● **CHILI AND SUGAR ARE GIVEN AS GUIDE QUANTITIES ONLY.**
VARY TO TASTE.
● **MEASURES FOR BEANS AND GRAINS REFER TO DRY INGREDIENTS.**

Man selling lychees, other fruit and vegetables, China. *Photo: Alain Le Garsmeur/Tony Stone Worldwide.*

MAURITIUS

Rum cake

Where you get sugar cane you almost certainly get rum, and Mauritius is no exception. Sugar cane was introduced by the Dutch; slaves to work the plantations were brought in from Mozambique and Madagascar.

Another Mauritian claim to fame is the extinct bird, the dodo. Apparently the dodo stayed so long in unpeopled Mauritius it forgot how to fly.

At all events, the ungainly bird was easy meat for the ravenous Dutch sailors who began arriving in the late 16th century, en route from the Cape to the Spice Islands (now Indonesia). Their name for it was *doudo* – simpleton. They were hungry too for the island's ebony forests and palm trees. When they left over a century later, the trees had almost gone and the large, flightless bird was dead as a....

INGREDIENTS

1¹/₂ cups / 180 g plain flour

4 eggs, beaten

³/₄ cup / 200 g sugar

¹/₄ pound / 110 g margarine

¹/₂ cup / 120 ml dark rum

1 tablespoon cornstarch/cornflour

¹/₄ teaspoon baking powder

grated zest and juice of 3 limes or 2 lemons

Heat oven to 350°F/180°C/Gas 4

1. First, grease an 8-inch/20-cm square cake tin. Sprinkle on some flour and then tap the tin to remove the excess.

2. Sift the flour together with the cornstarch/cornflour and baking powder into a bowl.

3. In another bowl, cream the margarine and sugar together. Then pour in the beaten eggs, a little at a time and stir continuously. If the mixture seems to be curdling, shake in a little of the flour. Continue until all the eggs are incorporated.

4. After this is done add the rum, grated rind and lime or lemon juice, again adding more flour as necessary. Combine into a smooth creamy mixture.

5. Now fold in the remaining flour and stir well. Then pour the mixture into the cake tin, smooth the top, and cook in the middle of the oven for about 1 hour. When it is ready, remove from the oven and leave it to cool in the tin ■

MYANMAR/BURMA

Semolina dessert

Serves 4

Awarded the Nobel Prize in 1991, Myanmar's Aung San Suu Kyi was kept a prisoner in her own home by the government. Her party, the National League for Democracy won a landslide victory in the 1990 elections, but the governing generals were not ready to give up their power.

Most of Myanmar's people live in the main rice-growing area, the central valley where the Irrawaddy, Sittang and Salween rivers flow. Three-fourths of the population are Burmese but the Karen, Kayan, Shan, Kashin and other groups have resisted domination by the Burmese majority.

INGREDIENTS

1 cup / 150 g semolina

2 tablespoons coconut milk

1-2 tablespoons sugar

seeds of 1 cardamom pod, crushed

2 tablespoons dried/desiccated coconut

2¹/₂ cups / 590 ml water or milk, or a mixture of the two

oil

1. Start by heating the oil in a wok or large pan and then put in the semolina. Stir it briskly for a few minutes until it begins to brown.

2. Reduce the heat now and pour in the coconut milk, mixing well, and continue to cook for 3-4 minutes.

3. At this point, put in the sugar and cardamom and stir again. Pour in the water and/or milk, adding more of these if needed to obtain the desired consistency. Serve hot with the desiccated coconut sprinkled on top ■

SRI LANKA

Bananas in arrack

Serves 2

'A typical Sri Lankan meal will consist of rice, local vegetables cooked with light spices, herbs and curry leaves, with a dessert of fresh fruit and the much celebrated Ceylon tea to follow.

'This is a special-occasion dessert from one of Sri Lanka's top chefs, Chang Cey Wen.' *Nalin Wijesekera, Mount Lavinia, Sri Lanka*

I N G R E D I E N T S

2 tablespoons margarine

2 ripe bananas, halved lengthwise

$1/3$ cup / 75 g brown sugar

seeds of 1 cardamom pod, crushed

juice of 1 lime

juice of 3 nectarines or 2 oranges

grated rind of 1 orange

$1/2$ teaspoon cinnamon

2 tablespoons arrack, brandy or red wine

1. Melt half the margarine in a pan and lightly sauté the bananas until they are golden and semi-cooked. Then lift them out carefully and set aside.

2. Now warm the rest of the margarine. Add the sugar and cardamom and stir continuously. When the sugar is dissolved, add the citrus juices and the orange rind. The sugar will caramelize as the juice hits it but it will liquify again later.

3. Cook this for a while until the liquid thickens, and then place the bananas in it.

4. Pour the arrack or brandy over the dish and set it aflame (if using red wine, this will not flame so just pour it over). Serve immediately with a sprinkling of cinnamon on top ■

Koti ciri (Cheetah milk cocktail)

Makes 2 drinks

'This is a cream cocktail, ideal as a long cool drink that could be garnished and served on a sultry day. The national drink is *arrack*, made predominantly with a base of coconut palm

toddy (alcohol) or imported molasses.' *Nalin Wijesekera, Mount Lavinia, Sri Lanka*

Arrack, used here, can also be made from the sap of the wild date palm and the palmyra palm. A type of sugar is also obtained from these plants.

I N G R E D I E N T S

1 egg yolk

$^1/_3$ cup / 80 ml arrack or dark rum

2 tablespoons sugar

zest of lime or lemon

1 clove

$^1/_4$ teaspoon grated nutmeg

$^2/_3$ cup / 160 ml cold milk

1. Put all the ingredients, except the milk, into a bowl or blender and whisk well.

2. Then pour in the chilled milk; whisk again and serve immediately ■

THAILAND

Khao niaw man (Rice dessert)

Serves 4

Thailand with its rapid economic growth and industrial expansion is moving into the 'little tigers' realm of Taiwan, South Korea, Hong Kong and Singapore. Integrated circuits join its list of exports, which include traditional agricultural items such as rice, tapioca (from cassava/manioc) and rubber.

Use short-grain, glutinous or pudding rice for this recipe, soaked for 1 hour.

I N G R E D I E N T S

$^1/_2$ cup / 110 g short-grain rice, soaked

1 tablespoon coconut milk powder

seeds from 1 green cardamom pod, crushed

sugar

1 tablespoon dried/desiccated coconut, toasted

salt

FOR THE SYRUP *

$^1/_2$ cup / 120 ml water

$^1/_2$ cup / 110 g sugar

* These two items are to make a syrup, but you could use ready-made syrup or clear honey instead.

1. Set a pan of water on to boil. Add the rice when it is boiling and cook for 10 minutes or so. Drain.

2. Turn the rice into a bowl and put in the coconut milk powder, cardamom seeds and sugar.

3. Add a pinch of salt and mix the ingredients well. Scatter the toasted coconut on top and serve as it is, or with syrup, below.

4. To make the syrup, dissolve the sugar in the water as you bring it to the boil. Then hard boil for 10-15 minutes until it thickens. Pour over the individual portions and serve hot or cold ■

BERMUDA

Corn/maize bread

Bermuda has the dubious distinction of being one of the oldest British colonies. King James I granted a charter to the Virginia Company to include Bermuda in the dominion in 1612, and the first settlers arrived soon afterwards. The islands were later sold to the City of London and became Crown property in 1684. Today the main earnings are from tourism and international business such as tax-free insurance companies.

This corn/maize bread is light and can be eaten on its own as a snack or as a side dish – it goes well with stews.

INGREDIENTS

$^1/_2$ cup / 70 g margarine, melted

$^1/_2$ cup / 110 g sugar

1 egg, beaten

1 cup / 125 g corn/maize meal

1 cup / 125 g flour

3 teaspoons baking powder

$^1/_2$ teaspoon nutmeg

1 cup / 240 ml milk

pinch of salt

Heat oven to 350°F/180°C/Gas 4

1. Mix the margarine and sugar together. Then add the egg and the corn/maize meal.

2. Next sift in the flour and baking powder. Now add the nutmeg and salt and pour in the milk, stirring to mix well.

3. When this is done, grease an 8-inch/20-cm square baking tin and spoon or pour the mixture into it. Bake for about 1 hour ■

BOLIVIA

Limeade

Makes 6-8 drinks

'This recipe comes from the tropical Beni region and makes an easy refreshing drink, perfect for hot weather. It comes through Sophia Tickell, a United Nations' Association volunteer, from when she travelled here.' *Linda Farthing, Cochabamba, Bolivia*

INGREDIENTS

5 limes or 3 lemons, unpeeled and roughly cut (remove pips)

sugar to taste

water to taste

1. Put the lime or lemon chunks with the sugar and water into a blender and liquidize.

2. Strain, add ice and serve ■

CARIBBEAN

Cassava/manioc pone (Cake)

An imaginative way to try cassava/manioc – a staple of the region. It is now also cultivated widely in other parts of the world, including Africa. Although it is starchy and low in protein, the plant's ease of cultivation and resistance to drought make it a popular crop.

The *pone* is crunchy on the outside while soft and chewy inside.

I N G R E D I E N T S

1 cup / 100 g dried cassava/manioc *

1 cup / 75 g dried/desiccated coconut or use fresh cooonut, grated

1 tablespoon margarlne

$^1/_2$ cup / 110 g sugar

1 teaspoon baking powder

$^1/_2$ teaspoon allspice, ground

$^1/_2$ teaspoon cinnamon

1 teaspoon vanilla essence

$^3/_4$ cup / 200 ml milk
$^3/_4$ cup / 200 ml water } mixed

* This is sometimes called gari. It is available in specialist shops selling Caribbean foods.

Heat oven to 375°F/190°C/Gas 5

1. Mix the dried cassava/manioc and the coconut together, and then cut in the margarine.

2. Next add the sugar, baking powder, allspice, cinnamon and vanilla essence. Pour in enough milk and water to make the ingredients bind and then leave the mixture to stand for 10 minutes or so to absorb the liquids. It should be soft but not runny.

3. Grease a shallow baking tin and pour the pone into it so that the mixture lies about 2 inches/5 cms deep.

4. Bake for approximately $1^1/_2$ hours or until the pone is crisp and brown. Turn it out and cut into squares – serve hot or cold ■

Baked bananas with molasses

Serves 4

Remember the Boston Tea Party, when the New World settlers resisted the British imposition of a tea tax in 1773? This was meant to be the act of resistance that sparked the war of independence. However some believe that the final schism was prompted by the Molasses Act, passed some 40 years earlier, which imposed a weighty tax on sugar and molasses coming from anywhere other than the British sugar islands of the Caribbean.

I N G R E D I E N T S

4 bananas, halved lengthwise

$^1/_2$ -1 tablespoon molasses or black treacle

juice of $^1/_2$ lime

$^1/_2$ teaspoon cinnamon

$^1/_2$ teaspoon allspice, ground

$^1/_2$ tablespoon grated orange rind

$^1/_2$ tablespoon sugar

a little margarine

1-2 tablespoons rum

Heat oven to 350°F/180°C/Gas 4

1. Grease a shallow ovenproof dish with the margarine and lay the banana halves in it. Spoon the molasses over them.

2. Combine the rest of the ingredients, except 1 tablespoon of the rum, in a small bowl and then pour the mixture over the bananas and molasses.

3. Bake for 10-15 minutes and when ready to serve, heat the remaining rum in a spoon over a flame until it ignites. Then quickly pour it over the bananas and serve immediately ■

> **IN ALL RECIPES**
> ● PEPPER AND SALT ARE TO TASTE.
> ● CHILI AND SUGAR ARE GIVEN AS GUIDE QUANTITIES ONLY.
> VARY TO TASTE.
> ● MEASURES FOR BEANS AND GRAINS REFER TO DRY INGREDIENTS.

BANANAS

*'You can put them in a salad
You can put them in a pie
Any way you want to eat them
It's impossible to beat them.'*

UNBEATABLE bananas, featured here in a US advertising jingle from the 1940s, came originally from South-East Asia. The plant was taken to West Africa by early traders, and by the fifteenth century it was a basic food there. Noting this, Portuguese and Spanish slave traders laid in stores of bananas for the Africans bound for the Americas. These may have been small red-skinned bananas rather than the large yellow ones we find in our shops today. Bananas come in many colors, sizes and degrees of sweetness, but few are as sweet or as suited for travelling to colder climes as the specially-bred types like *Gros Michel* or *Robusta*.

These big yellow varieties were developed in the nineteenth century, and 1804 is the first recorded year in which bananas landed in New York (from Havana). They soon made an impression as an exotic delicacy, so much so that in 1876 bananas were featured at the United States Centennial Exhibition in Philadelphia.

The trade was helped by the development of refrigerator ships which meant that early-picked fruits could travel great distances without perishing, and appear in our shops with their golden yellow skins suggesting sun and health.

In most of the world's warm and wet tropical parts, bananas are common plants, bringing a range of useful materials as well as food to local people. The 'trees', which can live for over 60 years, are really giant herbs and do not need much tending. Their fruits provide food for millions of people, whether as *fufu* – the mash found in East and West Africa and the Caribbean – or as *phalon ka chaat*, an Indian snack. All over the tropics the large dark green leaves serve as platters, as food wrapping and even as impromptu umbrellas; and everywhere bananas grow you will find a banana-based alcoholic drink or 'toddy' that helps ease away the day's problems.

Problems abound for workers on the world's banana plantations. Large companies such as United Brands (which owns Fyffes), Castle and Cooke (Dole), Del Monte and Geest have plantations or employ people working their own small farms in Panama, Honduras, Ecuador, St Lucia, St Vincent, Dominica, Surinam, Costa Rica, Colombia and the Philippines. The big companies demand perfect and unblemished fruit which means workers are exposed to all kinds of chemicals as the bananas are cosseted with fertilizers, pesticides and fungicides. 'The bananas are better loved and cared for than the workers,' says Connie Actub, a trade unionist in the Philippines.

The Philippines shot into banana exporting under the Marcos regime, and today 90 per cent of its exported fruit goes to Japan. The US is still the largest consumer at over two million tons a year ∎

CHILE

Manzanas asadas (Baked apples)

Serves 6

Chile's main alcoholic spirit is the powerful *pisco*, grape brandy, often served with lemon juice. *Chop* is the name for local draught beer, and the herbal tea, *yerba maté*, is common around the country. Wine is increasingly exported, as are Chilean grapes and apples.

I N G R E D I E N T S

6 large cooking apples, cored

4-6 tablespoons brown sugar

1¹/₄ cups / 300 ml red wine or sherry

1 stick cinnamon

yogurt or cream +

+ optional ingredient

Heat oven to 400°F/200°C/Gas 6

1. Pierce the apple skins and then place them in a greased ovenproof dish. Pile the sugar into the hollows.

2. Pour the wine or sherry into each apple, on and around them. Add the cinnamon stick and then put the dish into the oven for about 20-30 minutes until the apples are cooked. Serve with yogurt or cream ■

CUBA

Banana, rum and orange cocktail

Serves 2

The collapse of the Soviet Union has left Fidel Castro's Cuba without allies and with few active friends. It is a race against the clock to make the island more self-sufficient while retaining popular support. Sugar is still the largest source of foreign exchange, but without oil and fertilizer from the Soviet Union, the harvest will be well down on recent years.

The Caribbean islands abound in all kinds of fruit, sugar and rum, and there are lots of these knock-you-out drinks as a result…

I N G R E D I E N T S

1 banana, peeled and chopped

juice of 3 oranges or 1 cup / 240 ml orange juice

3 tablespoons rum

cracked ice

1. Mix the banana and orange juice together in a blender or beat with a whisk. Add the rum and pour over the cracked ice in a glass ■

Pineapple daiquiri

Serves 2

Another head-spinning drink…

I N G R E D I E N T S

1 cup / 240 ml fresh or cartoned pineapple juice

1 tablespoon orange liqueur

¹/₂ cup / 120 ml light rum

juice of ¹/₂ lime

sugar to taste

ice cubes

1. Place everything except the ice into a blender or beat well with a whisk.

2. Now put the ice cubes in a clean cloth and whack them with a rolling pin or hammer to crush the ice.

3. Heap the cracked ice into the glasses and pour the daiquiri over ■

HONDURAS

Dulce de leche (Milk dessert)

Serves 4-6

In the north of this Central American state lies Copán, a city of the former Mayan empire. The Florentine explorer, Amerigo Vespucci (from whose name we get America) was apparently the first European to reach Honduras and by 1498 it was conquered by Spain, despite fiery resistance from the Indians. Today it is a major producer of bananas and coffee.

This recipe needs a strong arm and patience; you stir for half an hour while the milk and ground almonds thicken together. It is sweet liquid, not unlike condensed milk, and can also be served in small bowls to accompany other desserts such as fruit salad.

I N G R E D I E N T S

3 cups / 700 ml milk

¹/₂ cup / 110 g sugar

2 tablespoons ground almonds

1 stick cinnamon

1. Pour the milk into a heavy saucepan and add the sugar, ground almonds and cinnamon. Bring to boiling point.

2. Cook over a medium heat, stirring all the time, for half an hour or so until the mixture thickens. Remove the stick of cinnamon before serving either warm or cold ∎

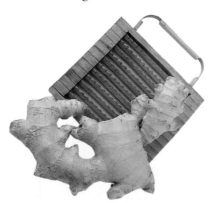

JAMAICA

Gingerbread

Arawak Indians lived on this island which they called 'Xamayca' (Jamaica) – land of springs. They had displaced the original inhabitants, the Guanahatebey, who had migrated there from North America. In the mid-16th century, Spanish historian Francisco López de Gomara was able to record that *'Jamaica resembles Haiti in all respects (as) here the Indians have also been wiped out.'* By 1547 ginger (used in this recipe) was established as a commercial crop in Jamaica, and it is still a major export along with rum, sugar and molasses.

I N G R E D I E N T S

1 teaspoon ground ginger

1¹/₂ cups / 180 g flour

¹/₂ cup / 50 g chopped mixed candied peel or sultanas

¹/₃ cup / 50 g margarine

1 tablespoon dark brown sugar

2 tablespoons molasses syrup or black treacle

¹/₂ teaspoon soda bicarbonate

2 tablespoons milk, warm

1 egg, beaten

Heat oven to 300°F/150°C/Gas 2

1. Using a large bowl, sift in the ground ginger with the flour and then mix in the peel.

2. Next heat the margarine, sugar and molasses over a low heat and stir until the sugar has dissolved.

3. When that is done, stir the soda bicarbonate into the warm milk. Add the egg and beat them all together for a few seconds.

4. Now add the molasses mixture and the egg and milk liquid to the flour, mixing thoroughly.

5. Line a bread tin with waxed/greaseproof paper or grease it well; pour in the cake mixture and bake for about 1 hour. Leave it to cool in the tin for 15 minutes or so before turning out. Serve cold ∎

MEXICO

Arroz de leche (Rice pudding)

Serves 4-5

Rice was introduced to the Americas, via Europe, probably in the 17th century and it is now widely grown all over the region. If you are British and rice pudding conjures up memories of unimaginative school dinners, then you may wish to pass this by. But don't – this rice pudding is something else, as they say.

I N G R E D I E N T S

1 cup / 240 ml water

rind of 1 lemon, grated

1/2 cup / 110 g rice

1 quart / 1 liter milk

1 stick cinnamon

1/2 cup / 110 g sugar

2 egg yolks, beaten

1/2 cup / 50 g sultanas or raisins

1 tablespoon margarine

1 teaspoon cinnamon

salt

1. Boil the cup of water together with the lemon rind and a little salt; put in the rice and cook until the water is absorbed and the rice is fluffy.

2. When this is done pour in the milk, add the stick of cinnamon and simmer gently for 10-15 minutes. Now put in the sugar and cook slowly for a further 10 minutes.

3. Remove the pan from the heat and add the egg yolks and sultanas or raisins, stirring as you do this.

4. When these ingredients have amalgamated, bring the saucepan back to the heat and bring the mixture just to boiling point.

5. Cook gently, stirring all the time, for 5 minutes more or until the mixture has the consistency of a custard. Put in the margarine and sprinkle the teaspoon of cinnamon over the top just before serving. Serve hot or cool ■

Fresh fruit salad

Serves 4

Mangoes, used here, come from south east Asia and are particularly popular in India where they are often turned into chutneys and desserts such as *aam ras* (p.143). The fruit is an good source of vitamin A.

This fruit salad tastes best served at room temperature.

I N G R E D I E N T S

2 mangoes

4 peaches

6 plums

1 cup / 100 g cherries, stoned

1 cup / 100 g strawberries

cream or yogurt +

+ optional ingredient

1. Wash and cut up the fruit into small pieces and serve with cream or yogurt if liked ■

Woman preparing meal, Wadi Chesaha, Yemen. *Photo: Maria Marechaux.*

tinue to simmer, turning from time to time until the pumpkin is cooked and has absorbed almost all the syrup.

3. Mix in the walnuts and then transfer the pumpkin to a serving dish and sprinkle the lemon juice over. Serve hot or cold with the cream or yogurt ∎

IRAQ

Walnut and pumpkin pudding

Serves 4

Iraq is one of the world's major exporters of dates but all agricultural production has suffered as a result of the war with Iran (1980-1988) and the 1991 Gulf War. Irrigation systems have been bombed, and the irrigated soils suffer from salination – saltiness which kills the plants. For unless there is perfect drainage, constant irrigation removes salts from the soil and concentrates them, destroying fertility. Barley, one of Iraq's main food crops, is more resistant to salinity than the other major grain there, wheat – but even barley cannot withstand it for ever.

I N G R E D I E N T S

¹/₂ cup / 110 g sugar

¹/₂ cup / 120 ml water

1 pound / 450 g pumpkin, cubed

¹/₃ cup / 30 g walnuts, chopped

1 tablespoon lemon juice

1 cup / 225 g cream or yogurt +

+ optional ingredient

1. To begin, make a syrup by dissolving the sugar in the water over a gentle heat. Then increase the temperature and boil hard for 5-10 minutes, stirring continuously, until the mixture thickens but does not yet caramelize.

2. Put the pumpkin cubes into the syrup and cook gently with the lid on for 1 minute. Then remove the cover and con-

IN ALL RECIPES
● PEPPER AND SALT ARE TO TASTE.
● CHILI AND SUGAR ARE GIVEN AS GUIDE QUANTITIES ONLY.
VARY TO TASTE.
● MEASURES FOR BEANS AND GRAINS REFER TO DRY INGREDIENTS.

LEBANON

Salatah faowakeh (Fruit salad)

Serves 4-6

'The year when there are plentiful dates and almonds, there is prosperity and long life,' goes a Lebanese saying. This dried fruit and nut salad is best made well in advance as it needs to stand in the refrigerator, or cool place, for about 3 hours, to let its flavors reach their full strength.

I N G R E D I E N T S

1-2 tablespoons clear honey

2 tablespoons mulberry or orange syrup, Van der Hum, Kirsch or Cointreau

1 cup / 240 ml cold tea

¹/₂ cup / 120 ml orange juice

2 tablespoons rose water

8 dried figs, cut into ¹/₂-inch/1.5-cm pieces

10-15 dried dates, stoned and halved

2 tablespoons sultanas or raisins

2 tablespoons whole hazelnuts

1 tablespoon whole almonds

2 tablespoons pistachio or cashew nuts

1 small melon or 2 peaches

1 orange, peeled and chopped

1 cup / 225 g yogurt or cream +

+ optional ingredient

1. Start by mixing the honey with the syrup or liqueur and blend in the cold tea, orange juice and rose water.

2. Now add the figs, dates, sultanas or raisins, hazelnuts, almonds and 1 tablespoon of the pistachio or cashew nuts. When these have combined well, put the bowl into the refrigerator and leave for 2 hours to soak.

3. After this, slice open the melon and discard the seeds. Cut the fruit into slices and then remove as much of the flesh as possible by dicing into cubes or small pieces. Add the melon

(or peaches if using) and the orange to the bowl of fruit and nuts and mix well. Return the fruit salad to the refrigerator for another hour.

4. Chop the remaining pistachio or cashew nuts and scatter them over the salad before serving with yogurt or cream ■

MIDDLE EAST

Almond crescents

Makes approximately 20

Almonds spread at an early stage from Asia to the Mediterranean region. They turn up also as sugared almonds, while ground almonds are used for marzipan and also frequently as a thickening agent for sauces or as flavoring in Arab cookery. With their many uses, almonds have the largest share of the world trade in nuts (peanuts are not included as they are legumes).

I N G R E D I E N T S

1¹/₂ cups / 110 g ground almonds

¹/₂ pound / 225 g margarine

2 tablespoons icing sugar

1 egg yolk

1 tablespoon brandy *

2 cups / 250 g flour

¹/₂ teaspoon baking powder

1 tablespoon sesame seeds

a few drops of almond essence

* Or use ¹/₂ teaspoon vanilla essence.

Heat oven to 325°F/160°C/Gas 3

1. Start by roasting the ground almonds on a baking sheet in the oven for about 10 minutes or until they turn a deeper golden shade.

2. While that is happening, cream the margarine in a bowl and then add the 2 tablespoons of icing sugar and the egg yolk. Mix well before stirring in the brandy or vanilla essence

Ayran (Yogurt drink)

Makes 1 cup

Milk starts fermenting quickly in a warm temperature, and given the right bacteria it can turn into pleasant and nutritious yogurt, rich in vitamin B_{12}. This is a Middle Eastern version of the Indian drink, *lassi*, cooling and delicious.

I N G R E D I E N T S

$^1/_2$ cup / 110 g yogurt

$^1/_2$ cup / 120 ml water or $^2/_3$ cup / 160 ml milk

pinch of dried mint

salt

1. Put the yogurt into a bowl and slowly pour in the water or milk, beating as you do so; or blend the ingredients.

2. Then add the mint and salt, mix well. Refrigerate before you serve the drink ■

and the ground almonds.

3. Sift the flour and baking powder into the almond mixture, combining the ingredients well with a wooden spoon.

4. Now take up walnut-sized pieces of the almond dough and form them into crescent shapes.

5. Press a few sesame seeds on top and then place them on a baking sheet and cook for about 30 minutes or until very lightly browned.

6. Remove them from the oven and leave to cool for a few minutes. Sift a little icing sugar over them if liked and then leave to cool completely before eating, or store in an air-tight container ■

MOROCCO

Fresh orange dessert

Serves 4-6

Morocco has two enclaves, Ceuta and Melilla. Melilla was founded by the Phoenicians and held by Romans, Goths and Arabs before the Spanish took possession in 1495. Ceuta was transferred to Spain in 1688. In 1956 Morocco recovered these two zones, but their ports still remain under Spanish control. Morocco's neighbor, the former colony of (Spanish) Western Sahara, was annexed by Morocco in 1976. But this met with resistance from the territory's inhabitants, the Sahrawis, who want self-determination. Over to the United Nations...

I N G R E D I E N T S

6 oranges, peeled

¹/₂-1 teaspoon ground cinnamon

2 teaspoons orange blossom water

icing sugar +

+ optional ingredient

1. Remove any pith from the oranges and slice them into thin rounds. Lay them on a flat plate and sprinkle on the icing sugar, cinnamon and orange blossom water.

2. Place in the refrigerator for 1 hour, but turn the slices over from time to time during that period. Serve with cinnamon biscuits (see below) ■

Cinnamon cookies/biscuits

Cakes and desserts feature prominently in Morocco's cafés and also in the pastry shops and street stalls. The most common are *cornes de gazelles* or *m'hencha* – almond-filled pastries covered with honey. The country produces grapes, melons, strawberries, peaches, figs and of course dates.

These are simple to make and very crumbly and delicious to eat, whether accompanied by tea, white wine or sherry or else served with a sweet such as the fresh orange dessert on this page.

I N G R E D I E N T S

2 cups / 250 g flour

¹/₂ cup / 120 ml oil

1 cup / 225 g sugar

rind of 1 lemon, grated

ground cinnamon

Heat oven to 350°F/180°C/Gas 4

1. To begin, grease and flour a baking sheet. Next sift the flour into a large bowl and then make a well in the center and pour in the oil. Add the sugar and lemon rind and mix well to form a dough.

2. Now take small balls of the dough and shape them into little flat round cookies. Place them on the baking sheet and sprinkle some cinnamon on top.

3. Bake for 20 minutes and then let them cool a little before eating ■

SYRIA

Ma'mounia (Semolina halva dessert)

Serves 4

Syria was once the name for the whole region between what is now Turkey and Sinai. The territory came under the control of Alexander 'the Great'. Later, its capital Damascus also became the capital of the Arab Empire. In the 11th century Europeans invaded during the Crusades; in the 16th century the country became part of the Ottoman (Turkish) empire. In this century the British and the French squabbled over control of the region, and it was not until 1946 that Syria became independent.

There are many versions of this halva dessert as it is popular all over the region.

INGREDIENTS

1 tablespoon margarine

1 cup / 150 g semolina

2¹/₂ cups / 590 ml milk (or half milk, half water)

¹/₂ cup / 110 g sugar

1 teaspoon ground cinnamon

1 tablespoon pignoles/pine nuts +

+ optional ingredient

1. Heat the margarine in a saucepan and add the semolina. Cook it gently and stir it round for about 5 minutes until it deepens in colour.

2. In a separate pan, bring the milk or milk and water to the boil with the sugar and then pour this gradually over the semolina. Stir over a low heat and cook until the mixture thickens.

3. When it is ready, set the pan aside, covered, for 15 minutes. And then serve it, cool, with cinnamon and the pignoles/pine nuts on top ■

Tunisia/Syria

Samsa (Almond pastries)

Makes about 20

These are usually made with *malsouqua* – a semolina pastry. Semolina is the hard grain obtained after milling wheat to make flour. You can use filo pastry instead for this recipe.

I N G R E D I E N T S

$^1/_2$ pound / 225 g ground almonds

$^1/_2$ cup / 110 g sugar

2 teaspoons grated orange peel

2 teaspoons ground cinnamon

$^1/_2$ pound / 225 g filo pastry

$^1/_4$ pound / 110 g margarine, melted

FOR THE SYRUP

juice of 1 lemon or lime

2 tablespoons geranium or rose water *

1 cup / 225 g castor sugar

1 $^1/_4$ cups / 300 ml water

1 tablespoon sesame seeds, toasted †

* Available in specialist and oriental grocery stores.

† To toast the sesame seeds, place them under the grill or broiler for a few minutes, shaking the tray frequently. They will turn a deeper shade.

Heat oven to 350°F/180°C/Gas 4

1. Place the ground almonds in a bowl and add the sugar, orange peel and cinnamon and combine well.

2. Grease a baking sheet and then cut filo pastry sheets into rectangles measuring 6 x 10 inches/15 x 25 cms, or cut them as required. Keep the remainder covered so that they do not become brittle. Brush each sheet with melted margarine as you use it.

3. Place a tablespoonful of the almond mixture on the end of the pastry strip. Next, fold the long sides inwards and then roll up the pastry into a cigar shape.

4. When this is done, arrange the cakes, seam side down, on the greased baking sheet and cook in the oven for 15-20 minutes until they are golden.

5. While they are baking, heat the water together with the rest of the sugar and cook, stirring until the sugar dissolves. Then add the lemon or lime juice.

6. Bring to the boil, stirring constantly, and hard boil for 15-20 minutes until the mixture thickens to make a syrup that coats the back of a spoon. Then sprinkle in the geranium or rose water and set aside.

7. When the pastries are baked, let them cool a little on a wire tray and then arrange them on a plate and pour the syrup over. Scatter the sesame seeds on top ∎

GLOSSARY

Fruit and vegetable stalls at St George's market, Grenada. Photo: Richard Bradbury/Tony Stone Worldwide.

GLOSSARY

A selection of some ingredients and other vegetarian items.
*See also **Notes to the Recipes** p.31, and introductions to individual recipes.*

Amaranth
A small grain, about the size of a poppy seed, amaranth was highly valued by the Aztecs of Central America.

Allspice
Named because it combines the flavor of several spices (cinnamon, cloves and nutmeg), allspice comes from the dried unripe berries of a small evergreen tree belonging to the myrtle family and native to tropical America. Most allspice is grown in Jamaica.

Arrowroot
Arrowroot powder, used as a thickening agent, is grown in tropical regions, and the main producer is St Vincent island in the Caribbean. The name may have come from the Arucu Indian name for it, *aru* root.

Asafoetida
Also known as **heeng**, this is a reddish dried gum resin with a strong smell and a garlicky flavor. It also aids digestion.

Bananas/plantains – *see also Featured Food p.152.*
Bananas probably originated in south east Asia and were taken to Madagascar and thence to Africa and the Americas. Varieties range from the red and yellow-skinned dessert types to the big green savory bananas or plantains, a staple in much of Africa and the Caribbean.

Beans, pulses and legumes – *see also Featured Foods on Beans p.68 and on Lentils p.94.*
Black beans, broad beans, haricot, lima or butter beans, pink, pinto, and red kidney beans originated in South America. Lentils are from the Mediterranean; black-eyed beans/cowpeas from Africa; pigeon peas from Africa or India; soybeans and azukis from China; chickpeas (garbanzos) and mung beans (green gram) from India and *ful medames* or brown beans from Egypt.

Bean-curd/tofu
Made from soybeans that have been cooked and puréed, then solidified into curds by the addition of vinegar and epsom salts, fresh bean-curd/tofu is white and custard-like and packed with protein. There are also smoked and fermented varieties such as *tempeh*.

Bulghur and cracked wheat
These are similar, both coming from wheat grains and both being very nutritious, but they are not the same. Both are staples in the Middle East. Bulghur is wheat that has been steamed and then dried before grinding whereas cracked wheat is uncooked wheat which has been dried and then cracked apart.

Caraway
The caraway plant is found from Europe to the Himalayas and its aromatic seeds have been used since early times, both medicinally as a remedy for flatulence, and as flavoring for bread, cakes, soups and the liqueur, *Kümmel*. Caraway seeds are sometimes confused with cumin because they look similar, but their taste is different and they should not be used interchangeably.

Corn/maize – *see also Featured Food p.116.*
The Americas' cereal contribution to the world's food supply, corn/maize is now grown widely in Africa and Asia as well.

Cassava/manioc
Of South American origin, cassava/manioc is now cultivated in many tropical

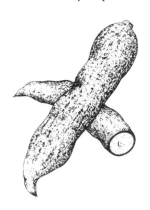

regions, and from it we also get tapioca. Although it is starchy and low in protein, it is easy to grow, and may be left in the ground after reaching maturity, without spoiling. It must always be boiled before eating as it contains toxins.

Cashew nuts

These grew originally in tropical America and were transplanted in Asia and Africa by the Portuguese and Spanish. The nuts grow on trees and make a curious sight as they hang from the bottom of the cashew 'apple'. After picking the nuts are roasted and then shelled by hand, a tedious process made worse as the shells contain an irritant. Kerala state in India, Mozambique and Tanzania are the main producers.

Cardamom

Cardamoms are the dried fruits of a herb related to the ginger family found in India and Sri Lanka. It is usually sold in pods which contain clusters of seeds.

Chilis and peppers

Chili peppers, together with cayenne, tabasco, paprika and sweet or bell peppers all come from the pod-like berry of various species of *capsicum* found in Latin America. Their spicy hotness arises from *capsaican* occurring in varying degrees in the different types. They were called

'pepper' because Columbus was looking for that spice and thought he had reached the East Indies rather than the Caribbean. When taken by the Europeans to Africa, India and Asia in the 16th century, chilis overtook regular pepper as the main condiment there. Chili powder, cayenne pepper or Tabasco sauce may be substituted for fresh or dried chilis.

Cilantro/coriander

The leaves and seeds of this plant are widely used in the Middle East (where it originated), Mexico, parts of Africa and Asia. The leaves resemble flat parsley and impart a strong flavor, while the seeds are mild and aromatic. The word coriander comes from the Greek for 'bug' referring either to the small bug-like seed, or to the fetid odor given off by the leaves.

Cinnamon

Cinnamon, used in curry powder and to flavor desserts, comes from the peeled bark of an evergreen tree native to Sri Lanka. For the best flavor,

buy it in its curled stick form. Cassia is often sold as cinnamon; it comes from Vietnam and has a stronger flavor.

Cloves

Cloves are the dried flower-buds of an Indonesian evergreen. Their export was a Dutch monopoly until plants were smuggled out in the 18th century, when Zanzibar and Pemba islands off East Africa became the leading producers. They are used to flavor meats and desserts, and in Indonesia to give aroma to cigarettes.

Coconut and coconut milk – *see also p.125.*

Originating in south east Asia, coconut palms provide leaves for roofing; coir (outer husk of the coconut) for matting; copra (the dried white flesh) used for cooking oil, soap, margarine and animal feed; the trees also give timber and shade; the coconuts give food, drink and are made into an alcoholic 'toddy'.

Cumin

Cumin or *jeera* is native to the eastern Mediterranean, but it has been cultivated also

for a long time in India and China. It comes from the dried fruit of a plant related to the parsley family. Either the whole seeds or the ground spice is used.

Curry leaves

The Tamil word for seasoned sauce is 'kari' from which we get 'curry'. Curry leaves, from India and Sri Lanka, look like

small bay leaves and when crushed release a curry fragrance. In the West usually only the dried leaves are found. Indonesian bay leaves, *daun salaam* can be substituted, or use curry powder instead.

Curry powder

A combination of spices which can be cooked in a little oil to bring out the full

flavor, curry powder usually includes turmeric, coriander seeds, black peppercorns, cloves, cumin seeds, cardamom, nutmeg, mace, cinnamon, ginger, chilis or cayenne powder, fenugreek, garlic, and mustard oil.

Dill

Dill comes from the Middle East and its anti-flatulence properties have ensured its popularity. Its pungent seeds are used as a pickling spice and for flavoring some Indian dishes. The milder feathery leaves are also used for aroma and decoration.

Fennel

Originating in southern Europe, fennel resembles dill in appearance. Its liquorice-

flavored seeds are an important spice, while the more delicately flavored leaves are used as a herb. The vegetable variety (Florence or Roman fennel) has aniseed-flavored leaf stalks which are good in salads, or they can be cooked as a vegetable.

Fenugreek

Native of the Mediterranean, fenugreek is related to clover. The plant is used as a vegetable while the seeds can spice curries.

Garam masala

A mix of spices ground to produce an aromatic flavoring for Indian foods, garam masala may include black pepper, coriander, cumin, cardamom, nutmeg, cloves and cinnamon. It is aromatic rather than hot.

Galangal/Laos powder

This Asian root imparts an intriguing flavor especially when cooked with coconut milk.

Ghee

Many Indian dishes call for ghee or clarified butter, which is made by gently heating butter to produce a clear liquid. This does not burn when frying, and as it has no milk solids it does not turn rancid. It is a saturated fat and you may prefer to substitute an unsaturated margarine or cooking oil.

Ginger

The knobbly ginger rhizome comes from south east Asia and is a popular ingredient there. The fresh 'root' is crunchy and strong in flavor. Dried ginger root and ground ginger do not have the same pungency, the quality that has

enhanced ginger's reputation as an aphrodisiac.

Granadillas – *see Passion fruit.*

Lemon grass

A lemon-flavored thick-stemmed grass that is widely used in south east Asia, lemon grass is often combined with the flavors of coconut, chili and ginger. Fresh lemon grass can sometimes be found, but it is more commonly available as dried in the West, from oriental stores.

Millet, teff and sorghum

One of the oldest cultivated foods, millet can grow in poor soils with little rainfall making it an invaluable resource in dry areas. Millet and sorghum, a similar crop, are the staple grains for over 400 million people in the world. Teff is grown in Ethiopia.

Miso

A fermented soy bean paste used as a seasoning and soup base. 'White' miso is made

with the addition of rice while 'red' miso incorporates barley and has a stronger flavor.

Molasses

Molasses is a by-product of sugar-cane refining and comes in differing strengths according to whether it is the first boiling (light), the second (darker) or the third (blackstrap). It is used to sweeten dishes such as Boston baked beans and to pour over pancakes.

Monosodium glutamate (MSG)

The white crystals, extracted from grains such as corn/maize and vegetables, have no special flavor of their own; they are meant to enhance the taste of the dish they are added to. MSG is an unnecessary additive and has been linked to unpleasant side-effects such as dizziness; it is a sodium-related (salt) item.

Noodles – *see also Featured Food p.124.*

There are buckwheat *soba*; 'cellophane' or 'shining' noodles made of ground mung or soy beans; noodles made of rice flour, potato flour, and seaweed. Egg noodles, made of wheat flour, are long and thin like shoe-laces.

Nutmeg and mace

These are both part of the same fruit of a tree native to

the Molucca Islands in Indonesia. Mace is the delicately-flavored red lacy covering encasing the stronger aromatic nutmeg seed. The main producers are Indonesia and Grenada.

Okra

One of Africa's indigenous vegetables and related to the cotton plant, okra travelled to the West Indies with the slave ships and is also widely used now in Caribbean as well as

in Indian cookery. The name okra comes from a Ghanaian Twi language word, *nkuruman*. Other names for the dark green pointed pod include *gumbo* (from Angolan *ngombo*), *bhindi* and *ladies' fingers*. When cooked, they become glutinous and help thicken soups and stews.

Orange blossom water and rose water

These essences, made from distilling fresh orange blossoms or rose petals, are used widely in the Middle East and

India to flavor drinks, pastries and desserts.

Panch phoron

Also called 'five mixed spices' this is made up of cumin, fennel, bayleaf, fenugreek and onion seeds.

Paprika – *see Chili peppers.*

Papaya or paw-paw

The papaya tree originated in tropical America and is now found in most tropical regions. The fruits resemble melons, with a cluster of black seeds in the middle. The leaves, latex from the fruit's skin and the fruit itself are used to tenderize meat, but mostly papaya is eaten as a fruit with a squeeze of lime.

Passion fruits or granadillas

Passion fruits grow on climbing plants found in South America. The flowers are used as a sedative while the fruits are eaten raw or used in icecream and fruit juice. One explanation of the name is that the Jesuit missionaries used the plant to illustrate the story of Jesus' death on the cross to the Indians.

Peanuts/groundnuts – *see also Featured Food p.42.*

see also Featured Food p.42.
These protein-rich 'nuts' are really legumes which originated in South America and were taken to West Africa. They are now grown more widely in Africa than the

indigenous Bambara groundnut (*njugo* bean) which, unlike peanuts, is not valued as an oilseed.

Pepper

Pepper, whose vines grow wild on the Malabar coast of south India, has been the most important spice in the world. Originally pepper was used in India to add pungency to curry powders – a function now mainly served by chilis which arrived from South America in the 16th century. Today it is grown in Asia, with India the largest exporter. White and black pepper are made from the same peppercorns but treated differently before grinding. For black pepper, unripe peppercorns are dried in the sun. White pepper results from soaking ripe peppercorns and removing the outer casing.

Pine nuts or pignoles

There are two main types of pine nut, the Mediterranean and the Chinese, the former being the more delicately flavored. These are the seeds from the cones of the Portuguese or stone pine tree. The nuts are eaten raw or roasted, and they are also used in confectionary especially in the Middle East.

Pistachios

These nuts grow on a small tree found in Central Asia. The green kernels are prized for their decorative color and fragrant flavor. They are eaten salted like peanuts, or incorporated into nougat and icecream. Turkey, Iran and the US are major producers.

Quinoa

A high-protein grain grown by the Incas in Peru and now increasingly popular in other parts of the world because of its food value and pleasant taste. Rinse well before use to remove slightly toxic saponin.

Rice

One of the world's oldest cultivated crops, today over 7,000 varieties are grown. It is the staple food that directly feeds most people: others such as corn are often fed to cattle or chickens for them to turn into food for humans. It has a lower protein content than other cereals, especially when it is stripped of its bran layer and polished to form white rice.

Saffron

The most expensive spice in the world comes from the dried style of a crocus. The best saffron comes from Spain, Turkey and India, adding delicate fragrance and vivid color to rice dishes. A Mexican variety, *azafran*, comes from safflower – a plant grown for its seeds which are made into oil.

Sago

These grains are made from the pith found in the stems of the sago palm which grows in Papua New Guinea, Malaysia and Thailand.

Sea vegetables

These are an important source of minerals such as iodine and B group vitamins. *Agar* and *carrageen* are used as setting agents instead of animal gelatine and seaweeds such as *nori*, *dulse*, *kombu*, *wakame* and *arame* make seasonings or side dishes.

Sorghum – *see Millet.*

Sesame seeds and tahina

Sesame seeds, *simsim* in some countries, are available in health food stores. They are rich in calcium and protein.

A staple in Asian cookery, the seeds are often roasted and used as a dipping sauce. In the Middle East the uncooked seeds are turned into a thick paste, *tahina*, which flavors the garbanzo/chickpea dip, hummus. The seeds are also used as decoration and in confectionary.

Soy sauce and tamari

There are many varieties of this sauce, used widely in Chinese and Japanese cooking. Made from fermented soybeans and wheat or barley, yeast and salt, the fragrant brown liquid comes as 'light' and 'dark' types. The dark one is enriched with caramel or molasses. Tamari is a mellow version.

Sweet potatoes

Widely grown in tropical regions, sweet potatoes came from South America – as did the round or 'Irish' potatoes we may be more familiar with. Cook them in the same way: they are delicious baked.

Tabasco – *see Chili peppers.*

Tamarind

The word comes from *tamar-i-hind* meaning 'the date of the East'. Tamarind is probably indigenous to Africa but was introduced into India in pre-historic times. The trees live for over 100 years and need little active managing. The pulp around the seeds give dishes an intriguing sourness, and the seeds yield a

glue as well as pectin and tartaric acid. Tamarind wood is hard and makes good charcoal.

Tahina – *see Sesame seeds.*

Tannias and taros

Tannias also known as yautia and 'new' cocoyams come from America while taros (called also eddoes, dasheen or 'old' cocoyam) are from south east Asia. Popular in tropical regions they are cooked like sweet potatoes.

Tempeh

This is an ancient Indonesian food, protein rich, usually made from fermented soy beans but also from other beans or grains. *Tempeh* is sold as cakes with the tastes and textures varying according to the ingredients and how long they are fermented for. Like bean-curd/tofu, it lends itself to other flavors.

Teff – *see Millet.*

Turmeric

Native to south east Asia, turmeric is a rhizome of the ginger family with a musty flavor and yellow coloring effect. It is used in many spicy dishes as well as to color rice, and for this purpose it is a cheaper option than saffron.

Vanilla

Vanilla, a popular flavoring for ice-cream and confectionary, comes from the pods of an orchid plant found in the Caribbean and Central America. Madagascar is the main producer.

Yams

These are underground tubers of vine-like plants. The Yellow or Guinea yam and the White yam are the West

African types while the Asiatic yam is found in south east Asia. An American variety is the 'cush-cush' yam. Although starchy, yams contain enough protein to make them a valuable part of the diet ■

INDEX

Seaweed gardens in Bali, Indonesia. *Photo: Christine Osborne Pictures.*

INDEX

BIBLIOGRAPHY

Animal Liberation Peter Singer (Thorson's, Wellingborough, UK, 1986)

Bananas, Beaches and Bases Cynthia Enloe (Pandora Press, London, 1989)

Diet for a Small Planet Frances Moore Lappé (Ballantine Books, New York, 1978)

Diet, Nutrition and the Prevention of Chronic Diseases Technical Report Series 797 (World Health Organization, Geneva, 1990)

Food First Frances Moore Lappé and Joseph Collins (Souvenir Press, London, 1980)

Food in History Reay Tannahill (Penguin, London, 1988)

Man and the Natural World Keith Thomas (Penguin, London, 1984)

Meat Nick Fiddes (Routledge, London, 1991)

Much Depends on Dinner Margaret Visser (Penguin, London, 1989)

Queer Gear Caroline Heal and Michael Allsop (Century Hutchinson, London, 1986)

The Animal Estate Harriet Ritvo (Penguin, London, 1987)

McCance and Widdowson's *The Composition of Food* A. A. Paul and D. A. T. Southgate (HMSO, London, 1979)

The Evolution of Crop Plants Edited by N. W. Simmonds (Longman Scientific and Technical, Harlow, 1986)

The Extended Circle compiled by Jon Wynne-Tyson (Centaur Press, Fontwell, 1985)

The Moral Status of Animals Stephen R. L. Clark (OUP, Oxford, 1984)

The Oxford Book of Food Plants G. B. Masefield, M. Wallis, S. G. Harrison and B. E. Nicholson (OUP, London, 1973)

The Right Way to Eat Miriam Polunin (J. M. Dent, London, 1984)

The Sexual Politics of Meat Carol J. Adams (Polity Press, Cambridge, 1990)

The Vegetarian Handbook Gary Null (St Martin's Press, New York, 1987)

The Vegetarian Handbook Jane Bowler (The Vegetarian Society, Parkdale, Dunham Road, Altrincham, Cheshire, WA14 4QG, 1990)

The Von Welanetz Guide to Ethnic Ingredients Diana and Paul Von Welanetz (Warner Books, New York, 1982)

Why You Don't Need Meat Peter Cox (Thorson's, Wellingborough, UK, 1986)

About the New Internationalist...

The New Internationalist (NI) is a monthly magazine produced by New Internationalist Publications Ltd, which is wholly owned by the New Internationalist Trust. New Internationalist Publications is a publishing co-operative based in Oxford, UK, with editorial and sales offices in Aotearoa/New Zealand, Australia and Canada.

The New Internationalist was started in 1972, originally with the backing of Oxfam and Christian Aid, but is now fully independent with some 70,000 subscribers worldwide. The NI magazine takes a different theme each month and gives a complete guide to that subject, be it Africa or feminism, the environment or food. The NI group also produces a Third World calendar, Almanac and Greetings Cards as well as Press Kits for the United Nations and occasional books and films.

For information write to:

Aotearoa/New Zealand P O Box 1905, Christchurch.

Australia and PNG P O Box 82, Fitzroy, Victoria 3065.

Canada and US 1011 Bloor Street West, Toronto, Ontario, M6H 1M1.

UK 55 Rectory Road, Oxford OX4 1BW.

About the author...

TROTH WELLS joined the NI team in 1972, helping to build up the subscription base. She now works mainly on the editorial side on NI magazines and projects such as the UNFPA State of World Population Report. In 1987 she took part in a project assessing the effectiveness of video in teaching with rural women in Kenya. She has travelled in Central America, Africa and South East Asia and in 1990 produced the **NI Food Book** - Recipes from Africa, Asia, the Caribbean and Latin America, and the Middle East.

PHOTO AND ILLUSTRATION REFERENCES

Color photos of various ingredients by *Mark Mason* and *Tayacan*. **Line drawings** by *Steve Weston, Brian Dear and Clive Offley*.

Black and white photos: 36 Ashanti ceremonial spoon and stamp, Ghana. 37 Water, Ghana, *Ian Berry/Magnum*. 39 Ndebele wall design, South Africa. 40 Family eating, Benin, *Claude Sauvageot*. 41 Woman with musical instrument, Topkapi Museum. 43 Chinese pictograph; Cultivating rice, China, *Marc Riboud/Magnum*. 45 Ferry, Hong Kong, *Dexter Tiranti/New Internationalist*; Indian wall hanging. 47 Indian wall hanging. 48 Children selling food, Indonesia, *Tina Tsukada*; Rubber plantation workers, Malaysia, *Dexter Tiranti/New Internationalist*. 51 Boy selling sweets, Dominican Republic, *Philip Wolmuth*. 52 Harvesting bananas, Dominica, *Philip Wolmuth*. 53 Fuelling the cooking stove, El Salvador *Peter Williams/Wings*. 55 Cylindrical stamp, Mexico. 56 Decorated stamp, Mexico. 57 Girl with vegetables, Cairo, Egypt, *Bror Karlsson/Panos Pictures*. 58 Shop in Cairo bazaar, Egypt, *Inge Morath/Magnum*. 59 Kurds making bread, Iraq, *William Carter/Camera Press*. 60 Islamic motif. 62 Women farmers, Ethiopia, *Mark Edwards/Still Pictures*. 63 Detail from Ethiopian magic scroll. 65 Ashanti bronze weight, Ghana. 66 Woman cooking, Ghana, *Werner Gartung*. 67 Women waving, Nairobi, Kenya, *Marian Kaplan*. 69 Health worker and women, Kenya, *Maggie Black/UNICEF*. 70 Unloading oats, Rwanda; Ndebele wall design, South Africa. 71 Trading *mielies* (corn/maize), Johannesburg, South Africa, *Orde Eliason/Link*. 74 Woman washing rice, Bangladesh, *Shahidul Alam/Drik*. 77 Pounding grain, India, *Claude Sauvageot*. 78, 79 Indian wall hangings. 80 Shadow puppet, Indonesia. 81 Malay women shopping, Penang, Malaysia, *Dexter Tiranti/New Internationalist*. 83 Kathmandu market, Nepal, *Jimmy Holmes/Panos Pictures*. 85 Rice field and temple, Sri Lanka, *Tomas Sennett/World Bank*. 87 Indian woman selling vegetables, La Paz, Bolivia, *Julio Etchart*. 88 Harvesting pepper, Amazonia, Brazil, *Mark Edwards/Still Pictures*. 91 Bead designs, Ecuador. 92 Cooking cassava/manioc fritters, Haiti, *Philip Wolmuth/Panos Pictures*. 93 Bird design motifs, Mexico. 95 Making tortillas, Yucatan, Mexico, *Hansruedi Dörig*. 96 Illustration from 'Nueva Coronica y Buen Gobierno', *Hansruedi Dörig*. Girls weeding lettuces, Peru, *UNICEF*. 97 Cosmetic spoon design, Egypt. 99 Harvesting in ancient Egypt, *Giraudon*; pyramids, Egypt, 1780, *Mary Evans Picture Library*. 100 Man drinking, Cairo, Egypt, *Jørgen Schytte/Still Pictures*. 101 Egyptian design. 102 Making tea, Saudi Arabia, *Camera Press*. 104 Bedouin preparing couscous, North Africa, 1890, *Mary Evans Picture Library*. 106 Detail from Ethiopian magic scroll; Winnowing, Ethiopia, *Chris Steele-Perkins/Magnum*. 107 Kikuyu wood dancing board, Kenya. 108 Village, Nigeria, *L F Kortenhorst/FAO*. 109 Coconut picker, Ghana, *Tina Tsukada*. 113 Harvesting peanuts/groundnuts, Senegal, *Werner Gartung*. 115 Woman winnowing with bamboo sieve, Bangladesh, *Shahidul Alam/Drik*. 117 Whampoa, China, *Mary Evans Picture Library*; man eating, China, *Gangfeng Wang/Panos Pictures*. 118 Woman and child, India, *Claude Sauvageot*. 122 Indian wall hanging. 123 Girls cooking rice, Sri Lanka, *Mark Edwards/Still Pictures*. 127 Fruit vendors en route to market, Haiti, *Julio Etchart/Reportage*. 128 Children selling potatoes and nuts, Guatemala, *Jørgen Schytte/Still Pictures*. 129 Aztec stamp design, Mexico. 130 Market, Oaxaca, Mexico, *Liba Taylor/Panos Pictures*. 131 Donkeys, Algeria, *Uri Urech*. 133 Wheatfield, Tunisia, *F. Botts/FAO*. 134 Making tea, Saudi Arabia, *Fred Peer/Camera Press*. 135 Youth and donkey, Tunisia, *Wolfgang Ziegler*. 136 Bedouin and camels, Jordan, *L. Giovenetti/FAO*. 138 Woman and baby, Cameroon, *Werner Gartung*. 139 Village, Uganda, *UNESCO/J. H. Blower*. 141 Ovambo women pounding corn, southern Africa, 1870, *Mary Evans Picture Library*; San cave painting, South Africa. 142 Man collecting date palm juice, Bangladesh, *Abu Naser Siddique/Drik*. 143 Fruits including papaya/pawpaw, bananas and breadfruit, *Hansruedi Dörig*; Women eating chapatis, India, *Claude Sauvageot*. 144 Girl eating rice, India, *Tina Tsukada*. 145 A nawab's mausoleum, India, *HMSO*. 147 Dodo, Mauritius. 148 Bananas, Uganda, *Jørgen Schytte/Still Pictures*; Schoolgirls with rice snacks, Sri Lanka, *Mark Edwards/Still Pictures*. 150 Man carrying quinoa grain, Bolivia, *Hansruedi Dörig*. 155 Family with girl making tortillas, Honduras, *Sean Sprague/Panos Pictures*. 157 Islamic motif; Crusaders' castle, Syria, *Mary Evans Picture Library*. 159 Making pitta bread, Iraqi-style, Israel, *Orde Eliason/Link*; Islamic motif. 160 Woman at vegetable market, Morocco, *Sean Sprague/Panos Pictures*. 161 Man with coffee pots, Saudi Arabia, *Fred Peer/Camera Press*; Islamic dish designs. 162 Koranic chapter markings.